AN INSTANT GUIDE TO

EDIBLE PLANTS

The most familiar edible wild plants
of North America
described and illustrated in full color

Pamela Forey and Cecilia Fitzsimons

CRESCENT BOOKS
NEW YORK • AVENEL, NEW JERSEY

Warning symbol

Throughout the book this sign has been used to indicate either that a plant has edible parts while the rest of it is toxic or that it may be mistaken for other plants which are poisonous and needs special care in identification.

If in any doubt DO NOT EAT!

Key to food uses

Can be eaten raw

Salad

Vegetable

Pickle

Soup

Fruit sauces, jams and jellies

Pies, muffins and pancakes

Syrup

Rice and Cereals

Flour

Seasoning

Candy

Tea, coffee or fruit drink

Wine or beer

Oil and butter

© 1989 Atlantis Publications Ltd.

This 1989 edition published by Crescent Books, distributed by Outlet Book Company, Inc., a Random House Company, 40 Engelhard Avenue, Avenel, New Jersey 07001.

Random House
New York • Toronto • London • Sydney • Auckland

Manufactured in Malaysia

ISBN 0-517-66217-5

10 9 8 7 6 5 4

Contents

Introduction

Using wild plants as foods, either on a camping trip or in the home, is becoming more and more popular. This book provides an introduction to edible wild plants, for people who have little knowledge of plants. It gives examples of all the ways in which plants can be used as foods, from salads to fruit pies, teas to root vegetables, and enables you to choose appropriate plants for all these uses.

The species of edible plants that we have selected are those most likely to be available to people who do not want to spend hours searching for a particular plant. They are all common and relatively easy to find. Some of them are weeds. We have not included edible plants that are endangered species or that are not found in sufficient numbers to justify their use. So, for example, you will not find included in this book, Spring Beauties or Trilliums, although both plants are edible. We would suggest that you do not use wild plants if they are not obviously common where you are collecting them.

Identifying Edible Plants

Identifying plants when you want to eat them is not as simple as identifying wildflowers, because most plants can be accurately identified only when in flower, and the edible parts of many plants are produced outside the flowering season.

Accurate identification of a plant that is going to be eaten is most important, since some edible plants are similar to poisonous ones (see section on poisonous plants.) The most foolproof method is to identify the plants accurately while they are in flower, and then to watch them through the seasons, so that you become familiar with, for example, the leaf rosettes of edible spring plants, the roots and tubers of edible winter plants and the fruits and nuts of edible fall plants.

How to use this book

The book is divided into five sections, depending on which part of the plant is edible. The sections are **Roots and Tubers**; **Leaves and Shoots**; **Buds and Flowers**; **Fruits**; **Nuts, Seeds and Miscellaneous**. Each section is identified by a different color band at the top of the page. There is an introductory page at the beginning of each section, summarizing the uses of these parts of the plant. Since a plant often has several edible parts, a cross reference is also provided. For example in the introduction to *Roots and Tubers*, all plants with edible roots or tubers from other sections of the book are listed.

First decide what use you want to make of the plant. Perhaps you want to make a salad, or a fruit pie, or a drink. The following paragraphs provide a summary of the uses to which each part of the plant can be put. Once you have found your requirements, you can turn to the relevant section(s). It is best to turn initially to the introduction on the first page of each section, which will provide further information.

Roots and Tubers

are most often used as vegetables or in salads. Familiar cultivated examples are potatoes, carrots and beets. They may be boiled, roasted or baked, or used as a thickening for soups. Some can be grated or chopped into salads; others may be roasted and ground to make coffee; others can be ground into flour. Some can be pickled. **14–29**

Leaves and Shoots

(the young growing tips and the first sprouts that appear in spring) can be used raw in salads, or cooked as green vegetables and pot-herbs. Familiar cultivated examples are lettuce, asparagus and red cabbage. The leaves of some plants, like New Jersey Tea, make good tea. **30–65**

Buds and Flowers

may be used as vegetables like broccoli, included in salads, made into fritters or candied. Other flowers are used to make drinks and wine. **66–67**

Fruits

may be eaten raw or dried for storage, used to make sauces, jams and jellies, baked into pies, muffins and pancakes. Familiar cultivated examples are strawberries, apples and cherries. Many can also be crushed to make drinks and some can be fermented to make wines. **68–97**

Nuts, Seeds and Miscellaneous

Nuts can be eaten raw like walnuts, ground into meal or pressed to extract their oils. They may be salted or candied, used in pies and cakes, mixed with cereals or added to salads.

Seeds may be eaten raw or roasted, ground into flour, added to cereals, used as a seasoning or as a flavoring in baking. Familiar cultivated examples include sunflower seeds, wheat and caraway. Some, like peas and beans, are eaten as vegetables.

At the end of this section we have featured a few plants that are difficult to categorize. Some of them, like Cat-tails, are important multiple use food plants, that have many useful parts; others, like the Sugar Maple, provide a special kind of food (its sap is made into maple syrup.) **98–121**

What's on a page

Most pages are devoted to a single species of plant but on some pages a group of plants is described, and one representative species is illustrated. There are four boxes of information on each page. The characteristic features of the plant are described in the first box, its habitat and distribution in the second, its uses as a food in the third and any similar edible or poisonous species in the fourth.

Characteristics of your plant

Plants can rarely be identified by a single feature. It is usually the combination of flower type, flower arrangement, leaf shape and leaf arrangement that tells you this is the right one. The information in the first box together with the illustration will help you to identify the plant. Accurate identification is essential; **if you are in any doubt, do not eat the plant**, for some species are deadly poisonous.

Habitat and distribution

The area and habitat in which any particular plant is found often provides important clues to its identity. The distribution map (see Fig. 1) will enable you to see at a glance whether the plant occurs in your part of North America. The second box on each page provides additional information about its habitat and distribution; a plant may not be present throughout its whole range but will be restricted to suitable habitats.

Fig. 1 Distribution map

● Commonly found in these areas

○ Partial distribution only

Food uses of the plant

In the colored band at the top of the page, the season when the plant can be harvested is given. In the third box, details are given on which parts of this particular plant are edible and how they can be used, in salads, pies, as vegetables etc. Symbols at the foot of the page provide a quick reference to the uses of the plant (**see page 6 for key.**)

In addition, a warning is given when only part of the plant is edible and other parts are poisonous. (**See Section on Poisonous Plants.**)

Similar edible or poisonous plants

In the fourth box, similar or related edible plants are described. Their food uses may be similar or quite different. Unrelated plants, that grow in similar habitats to the featured plant but that have similar uses, may also be described here. In addition, warnings are included in this box about similar or related poisonous plants that may be mistaken for the featured plant. It is important to note this information.

Poisonous plants ☠

Many plants are not edible and some are extremely poisonous. Some have edible parts, while the rest of the plant is poisonous. A warning sign is included in the illustration when a plant needs to be treated with caution (see page 6.) This may be for one of two reasons. In some plants, like *May Apple* and *Asparagus*, only a specific part of the plant is edible while the rest is poisonous and must be avoided. Other plants, like *Common Milkweed* and *Cow Parsnip*, have similar relatives which are poisonous, so accurate identification of these plants is essential and they are best avoided by beginners. In any event, it is **always** advisable to be sure of your identification. **If you are not sure that you have identified a plant accurately, do not eat it!**

Fig. 2 Specimen page

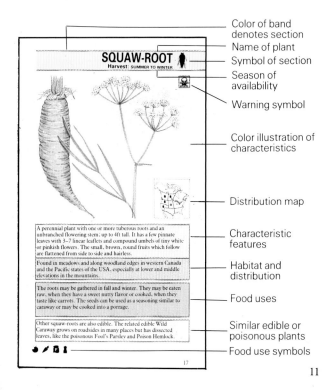

Color of band denotes section

Name of plant

Symbol of section

Season of availability

Warning symbol

Color illustration of characteristics

Distribution map

Characteristic features

Habitat and distribution

Food uses

Similar edible or poisonous plants

Food use symbols

Within the illustration:

SQUAW-ROOT 🔱
Harvest: SUMMER TO WINTER

A perennial plant with one or more tuberous roots and an unbranched flowering stem, up to 4ft tall. It has a few pinnate leaves with 3–7 linear leaflets and compound umbels of tiny white or pinkish flowers. The small, brown, round fruits which follow are flattened from side to side and hairless.

Found in meadows and along woodland edges in western Canada and the Pacific states of the USA, especially at lower and middle elevations in the mountains.

The roots may be gathered in fall and winter. They may be eaten raw, when they have a sweet nutty flavor or cooked, when they taste like carrots. The seeds can be used as a seasoning similar to caraway or may be cooked into a porrage.

Other squaw-roots are also edible. The related edible Wild Caraway grows on roadsides in many places but has dissected leaves, like the poisonous Fool's Parsley and Poison Hemlock.

17

11

Glossary

Annual A plant which grows from a seed, flowers, sets seed and dies in one year.

Axil The more-or-less V-shaped angle made by the junction between a leaf and a stem or twig.

Biennial A plant which forms leaves in the first year, produces a flowering shoot in the second year, flowers, sets seed and dies.

Bract A green leaf-like structure which has a flower in its axil, and which may remain on the plant with the fruit. Bracts vary enormously in size, shape and function.

Flower Structure

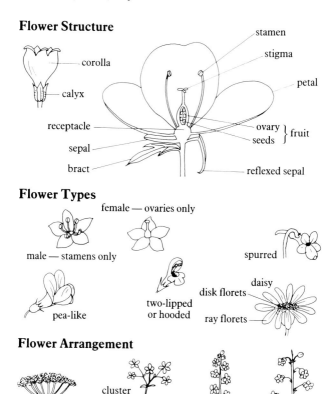

corolla

calyx

receptacle

sepal

bract

stamen

stigma

petal

ovary
seeds
} fruit

reflexed sepal

Flower Types

female — ovaries only

male — stamens only

spurred

pea-like

two-lipped or hooded

daisy

disk florets

ray florets

Flower Arrangement

umbel

cluster

spike

spray

Leaf Types

Simple leaves (not divided into leaflets)

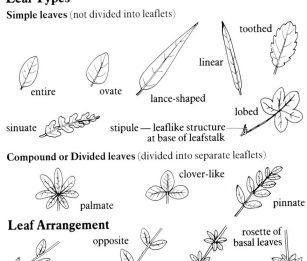

entire

ovate

lance-shaped

linear

toothed

lobed

sinuate

stipule — leaflike structure at base of leafstalk

Compound or Divided leaves (divided into separate leaflets)

palmate

clover-like

pinnate

Leaf Arrangement

opposite

rosette of basal leaves

alternate

whorled

Catkin A drooping spike of small flowers characteristic of some deciduous trees. Male catkins produce pollen; female catkins are pollinated and then develop into fruiting catkins which bear seeds.

Fruits contain the seeds. Different kinds of fruits include: **Berry** — a juicy fruit which usually contains several seeds; **Capsule** — a dry or fleshy fruit which splits open to release the seeds; **Nutlet** — a hard dry fruit containing a single seed; **Pod** — a long dry fruit, usually containing several large seeds, which splits open along one or both seams to release the seeds.

Node A point on a stem at which leaves are produced.

Perennial A plant which lives from year to year, starting into growth again each spring. Some perennial plants are herbaceous and die down each year, remaining dormant beneath the ground throughout the winter. Others are trees or shrubs; some lose their leaves in winter (**deciduous trees**), while others retain their leaves throughout the year and their growth slows down in winter (**evergreen trees**).

Shoot A new young growth.

Succulent Crisp and juicy or soft and juicy.

Tuber A swollen root or underground stem, which forms a food store for the plant.

Swollen roots & tubers (underground stems which resemble swollen roots) are food stores for the plant, often high in carbohydrates. They may provide an excellent source of wild food.

They are most often used as vegetables & can be cooked in many ways; most often they are boiled, roasted or baked. Some plants, like Groundnut, have roots that can be ground into flour; others can be added to soups. Some, like Dandelion & Chicory, have roots that can be roasted & ground as a coffee substitute.

As well as the plants included in this section, other plants in this book which have edible roots or tubers are:

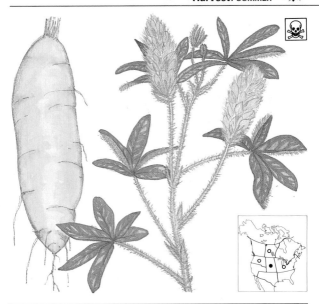

A perennial plant with a very swollen taproot. It grows up to 15in tall and is a bushy plant, with branched hairy stems and palmate leaves on long stalks. Each leaf has five leaflets. The flowers are blue and pea-like, growing in a dense spike and are followed by small, long-beaked pods with brown seeds.

Found in prairies, on dry banks and rocky slopes, in the prairie states of the USA and in the southern areas of the western Canadian prairies.

The plants with their taproots can be found in early summer but the upper parts disappear later, making the roots difficult to find. The roots can be boiled or baked like potatoes. They can also be dried for storage and ground into meal.

Related species, like the Scurf Pea, should not be eaten as they are poisonous to horses and cattle.

BURDOCK

Harvest: SPRING TO FALL

A branched, bushy biennial plant, up to 5ft tall, with a long taproot. The alternate leaves are oval and have hollow stalks; they are dark green with woolly undersides. The many, solitary purple flower heads are cupped by many green hooked bracts. These remain to form part of the hooked fruits.

Found on roadsides and in disturbed ground, waste places and fields across the USA and southern Canada but not found in extreme south or north. Introduced from Europe.

Roots of first year plants may be dug in late summer and fall. Peel and boil them, serve with butter; or cut them into strips and boil them dry with a dash of soy sauce. The roots can also be used to make beer. The flower stalks can be peeled and eaten like celery. Young leaves can be used in salads.

Great Burdock is a similar plant; its roots and leaves can be used in the same way. It has solid leaf stalks and these can be peeled and eaten raw, or boiled.

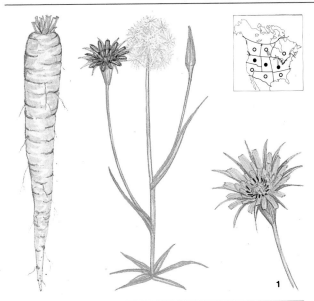

1

A biennial plant with a clump of lance-shaped leaves and a long fleshy taproot in the first year, and an erect leafy flowering stem, up to 3ft tall, in the second. The plant is full of milky juice. The solitary purple flower heads are followed by globular seed heads of seeds with parachutes.

Found on roadsides, along railroads and on disturbed ground, in old gardens and fields. Introduced into cultivation from Europe and now widely naturalized.

Dig the taproots in late summer or fall from first year plants, wash and peel and cook immediately, either fry in breadcrumbs or boil. The roots can also be roasted and ground as a coffee substitute. The young basal leaves can be used as salad greens or as a vegetable.

The related **Goat's Beards (1)** have yellow flowers but are otherwise very similar. They can be used in the same ways.

DAY LILY
Harvest: SPRING TO FALL

A large perennial plant with underground tubers and a clump of long, sword-like leaves, about 5ft tall. The tawny orange, funnel-shaped flowers grow in terminal clusters on long leafless stalks. They open a few at a time, each one lasting for a day, from elongated buds. The fruits are fleshy capsules.

A garden escape growing wild on roadsides, in vacant lots and on waste ground. Eastern USA and southern Canada, from Ontario southwards, west to Kansas and Texas.

Use young crisp tubers raw in salads or boil and eat like potatoes. Young shoots can be prepared like asparagus. Buds can be cooked and eaten like green beans or dipped with the flowers into batter and made into fritters. Fresh or dried buds and flowers can also be used in soups.

No similar edible species. Iris leaves (which are poisonous) are stiff, those of Day Lily are soft and arch over at the tips.

CHUFA

Harvest: ALL YEAR

A perennial plant with a clump of pale green, grass-like leaves around triangular flower-bearing stems. Thin underground stems with round tubers radiate outwards from the clump. The flowers are clusters of feathery spikelets and are followed by tiny yellowish, triangular nutlets.

Found along the margins of ponds and streams, low-lying damp ground and wet waste places. It may become a weed in some places. Southeastern Canada and throughout the USA.

The edible tubers can be eaten raw or boiled. They can also be dried and then ground into flour for use with wheat flour. Roasted and ground, they make a good coffee substitute. If they are soaked for two days, then mashed, the liquid can be sweetened and used as a drink.

Several other similar related plants have edible tubers which can be used in the same way.

BUGLEWEED
Harvest: FALL TO SPRING

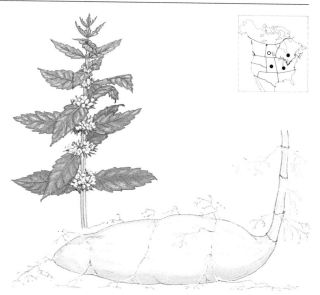

A perennial plant, up to 3ft tall, with upright hairless stems and opposite, lance-shaped, pale green leaves. The tiny white flowers grow in whorled clusters in the axils of the upper leaves. The fruits are tiny nutlets.

Found in low wet ground in the north and in mountain bogs and woods in the south of its range. Occurs east of the Rockies in southern Canada, southward to Oklahoma and the Dakotas.

Dig tubers from close to bases of the old withered stalks, wash and peel. They are crisp and can be added sliced to salads, pickled or boiled and served with butter.

Most species of this genus lack tubers. However one similar species, which grows in sandy areas on the east coast, does have tubers.

24

JERUSALEM ARTICHOKE

Harvest: FALL TO SPRING

A spreading, perennial plant which forms fleshy underground tubers. From these grow rough, hairy stems, up to 10ft tall, with large, rough, leathery, spearhead-shaped leaves. The several flower heads are like small sunflowers, about an inch across, with yellow ray florets and a yellow center.

Found in waste ground and on roadsides, in fields and damp thickets. Often cultivated. In northeastern USA and along the Canadian border, west to North Dakota and south to Tennessee.

Harvest the tubers from the first frosts of fall, throughout the winter. The tubers can be substituted for potatoes in any potato recipe. They can also be sliced raw into salads or boiled briefly and pickled.

Jerusalem Artichoke belongs to the same group of plants as **sunflowers**. Other sunflowers do not have edible tubers but do have edible seeds.

ARROWHEAD

Harvest: FALL TO SPRING

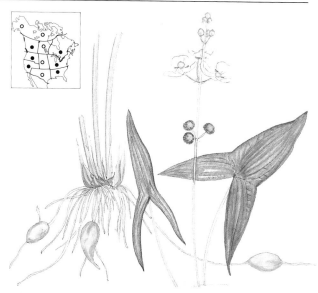

An erect perennial plant, about 3ft tall, with a clump of arrow-shaped leaves. The white flowers have three petals, and are borne in whorls of three along leafless flower stalks. On the fibrous roots grow small potato-like tubers, sometimes called duck potatoes.

Found in water at the margins of ponds and streams, in marshes and ditches throughout southern Canada and the USA but less common in the far north and south. Tubers grow in the mud.

Gather tubers whenever the water is not covered in ice, by loosening them from the mud with a rake or hoe. Bake or boil them like potatoes, but peel them after cooking. They can be used instead of potatoes in any potato recipe.

There are several other arrowhead species which also have edible tubers. They vary in the shape of their leaves, which may be narrow or broad.

INDIAN CUCUMBER

Harvest: SUMMER

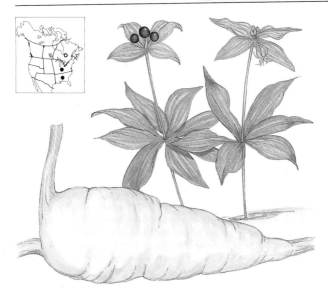

A perennial plant with upright stems, up to 2ft tall, bearing two whorls of simple parallel-veined leaves. A cluster of yellow-green flowers at the top of the stem is followed by inedible purple berries. Underground stems form swollen white edible tubers.

Found in moist woods and along the edges of swamps throughout eastern USA, west to Kansas.

The edible tubers may be gathered in summer, but should only be used when abundant, as digging up the tubers destroys the plant. Wash and eat the tubers raw or in salads; they can also be pickled.

No similar edible species. The inedible Starflower can be distinguished by the network of veins on its leaves.

27

GROUNDNUT

Harvest: ALL YEAR

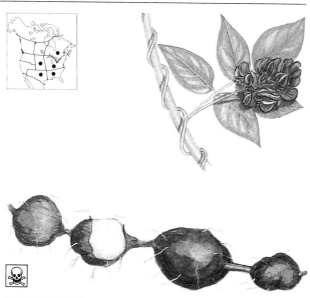

A perennial vine with underground fleshy tubers growing in a row. It has white stems with milky juice and large, pinnate leaves with 5–7 oval leaflets. Clusters of red-brown, pea-like flowers grow in the leaf axils and are followed by clusters of dry pods. These twist as they open to expose several seeds.

Found in moist woods and bottomlands, in thickets and on stream banks. Occurs in the USA east of the Rockies and in eastern Canada.

Dig up the row of tubers, working along the root to obtain all of them. Wash and peel and boil like turnips. They can also be sliced and fried, baked or roasted. The pods (although rarely abundant) can be roasted, seeds removed and fried in oil.

A similar species with only one tuber on the root, occurs in eastern states. The related vetchlings, locoweeds and milk vetches are poisonous.

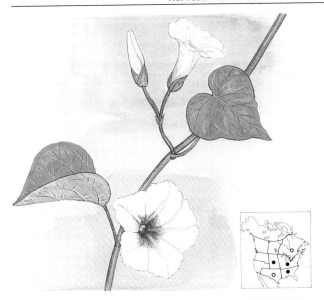

A perennial trailing plant, up to 12ft long, with large heart-shaped leaves and white, funnel-shaped flowers. The flowers may have a purple throat. The fruits which follow the flowers are two-chambered capsules.

Found in fields, along roadsides and fence rows, in dry sandy soil. Occurs in eastern USA west to Kansas and south to Texas.

The roots form large vertical tubers, like yams. They can be peeled and boiled, or baked like sweet potatoes. Serve with butter and seasonings.

Bush Morning Glory is a related bush-like prairie plant with purple flowers. Its large root tubers are also edible.

🌿 LEAVES & SHOOTS

Leaves & shoots (the young growing tips & the first sprouts that appear in spring) can be used in salads, as green vegetables or as pot-herbs. Since they quickly lose their taste & texture after picking, they are best used at once. They are high in vitamins & minerals; to retain these essential elements, leaves and shoots are best eaten raw or lightly cooked (except where cooking is essential to render them palatable or safe, e.g. milkweeds.) The leaves of some plants, like New Jersey Tea and Bergamot, make good tea.

As well as those in this section, other plants in this book, which have edible leaves or shoots include:

An annual plant which forms small clumps of weak, leafy shoots with loose terminal clusters of white flowers. The ovate leaves are borne in opposite pairs. There is a single line of hairs running along the stem from one node to the next. Each flower has five white, deeply notched petals.

A common weed introduced from Europe, which grows in cultivated land, in yards, on roadsides, especially in damp soil. Found throughout the USA and Canada.

Available throughout the year in southern regions but only in spring and summer further north. Young plants form an excellent salad green, rich in Vitamin C. It can also be cooked as a green vegetable, needing only 2 minutes cooking.

Other Chickweeds are also edible. Mouse-ear Chickweeds have hairy leaves and should always be cooked.

WINTER CRESS

Harvest: FALL TO SPRING

A biennial or perennial plant, with a rosette of leaves in winter and a branched erect stem in spring, up to 30in tall. The lower stem leaves are large and lobed, upper ones much smaller. Cylindrical clusters of yellow four-petalled flowers are followed by long narrow pods which split open lengthwise.

Found in wet meadows and ditches, on damp roadsides and waste ground. Widespread throughout N. America. Introduced from Europe.

A valuable winter source of vitamin C. Gather rosette leaves in frosty winter weather until they become bitter in spring. They can also be covered and blanched, when they lose their bitterness. They are good raw in salads or cooked as a green vegetable. Buds and flowers can be used like broccoli.

The leaves and flowers of the related and similar **Wild Mustard** can be used in the same way.

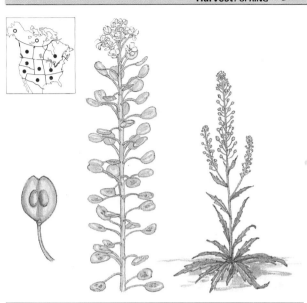
An annual or biennial plant with a basal rosette of lobed or dissected leaves and an erect leafy stem, up to 20in tall. There are several clusters of white, four-petalled flowers which elongate as they get older. The fruits are almost circular, notched pods borne on long stalks.

Found in disturbed and waste ground, on roadsides and in fields throughout much of N. America. Introduced from Europe.

Young shoots and leaves can be used in small quantities in salads or larger amounts boiled in two changes of water as a green vegetable. The seeds can be used as a seasoning in stews and soups.

Mustard, Field Cress and Shepherd's Purse are related weeds which can be used in the same ways. Field Cress is similar to Peppergrass; Shepherd's Purse has heart-shaped fruits.

Harvest: ALL YEAR

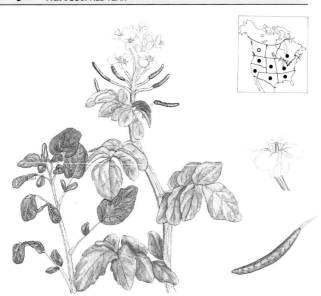

Succulent perennial plant with weak stems which root at the nodes and then turn upwards to form leafy shoots. Alternate leaves are compound, dark green. White flowers have four petals, borne in loose erect spikes. Fruits are slender pods, borne more or less upright with two rows of seeds inside.

Found in running water, streams and springs throughout the USA. European alien, widely grown and naturalized.

Collect young growth from unpolluted water. Cook like spinach or make into watercress soup with potatoes. Perhaps best used in salads; it has a peppery taste and should be combined with other milder green salad leaves. Rich in Vitamin C and minerals.

American Brooklime grows in similar places and can be used like watercress. It has succulent, creeping stems, opposite leaves and spikes of violet, four-petalled flowers.

A creeping perennial plant, up to 3ft tall, with weak, hairless, succulent stems which root at the base. The opposite leaves are oval, with pointed tips and toothed margins. Tiny, blue-violet flowers grow in loose spikes in upper leaf axils and are followed by small capsules in persistent calyces.

Found along streams and in springs, in swamps and ponds throughout the USA and much of southern Canada.

Gather young leaves and stems from unpolluted water and use like watercress in green salads. It has a bitter flavor and is best mixed with less pungent greens. It can also be used as a potherb.

Several related species (speedwells) may be used in the same way. **Watercress** grows in the same places and is also used in salads; it has white flowers and is not related to Brooklime.

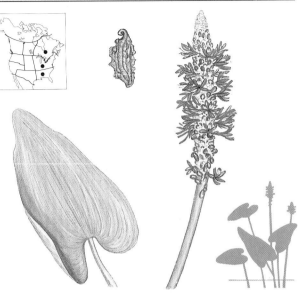

An aquatic perennial plant, about 3ft tall, with spreading beds of large, heart-shaped leaves which grow on long stalks and project above the surface of the water. The blue, two-lipped, funnel-shaped flowers are borne in dense spikes. The fruits are stiff capsules enclosed in the flower remains.

Found in the shallow water of marshes and along the margins of ponds, lakes and slow-moving streams in the eastern areas of southern Canada and eastern USA.

Pick the young leafstalks in early summer, before the leaves are fully opened, and chop them into salads or cook them as a green vegetable. The single seeds inside each fruit can be eaten as trail snacks, added to cereals or ground into flour.

Water Hyacinth is a floating plant with blue flowers, from southeastern USA. Its young leaves can be boiled or fried, but it may cause allergic reaction and should not be eaten raw.

MINER'S LETTUCE

Harvest: SPRING AND SUMMER

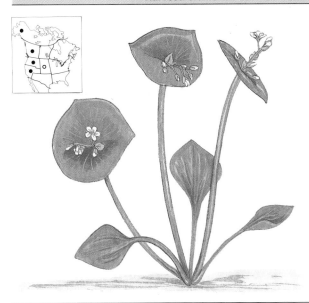

A small annual succulent plant, up to 15in tall. It has a clump of long-stalked basal leaves and many distinctive flowering stalks. Each flowering stalk has two leaves near the top, fused together across the stem into a circular disk, and a spray of small white flowers growing from the disk.

Found in moist places in gardens, woods and valleys, near springs and on lower mountain slopes, in the midwest and west of the Rockies in the USA, west of the mountains in Canada.

Young stems, leaves and flowers can be used in salads or just eaten raw; they are a good source of Vitamin C. They can also be cooked in a little water as a vegetable. The roots may be boiled lightly and taste a little like water chestnuts.

Siberian Miner's Lettuce is a larger plant without the disk-like leaves and with pink-striped flowers. It grows west of the northern Rockies and can be used in the same way.

PURSLANE
Harvest: SUMMER

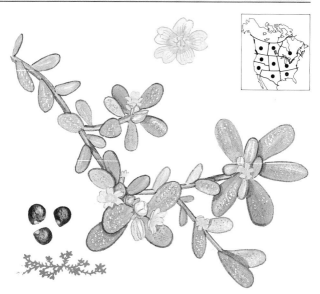

A mat-forming annual plant with many succulent, prostrate branches and opposite leaves. The leaves are shiny, fleshy and paddle-shaped, the terminal ones borne in rosettes. The yellow flowers are borne singly in the terminal rosettes and only open in sun. The fruits are egg-shaped capsules.

Found in waste places and fields and also as a garden weed throughout the USA and southern Canada. Introduced from Europe.

Pick and wash young shoots throughout the summer and use raw in salads or cook as a green vegetable. The stems can be pickled like cucumbers. Seeds can be ground and used as a flour. To gather them, dry the plants on sheets for a week, then shake the plants and store the seeds in paper.

Several related similar plants can be used in the same way.

CORNSALAD

Harvest: SPRING AND FALL

A weak, slender annual plant which forms small rosettes of leaves in the fall and flowering stems in the spring. The flowering stems are brittle and much branched, about one foot tall and with opposite, oblong leaves. The small, pale lilac flowers grow in flat clusters on forked branches.

Found in waste ground, on roadsides and cultivated land, usually on dry soils, in eastern and western USA and Canada, but not in the midwest or southern deserts.

Gather leaves from the rosettes in fall, and new leaves in spring. They are very good in a green salad or cooked as a vegetable, like spinach. They can also be made into soup with chervil.

Other similar Cornsalad species also have edible leaves.

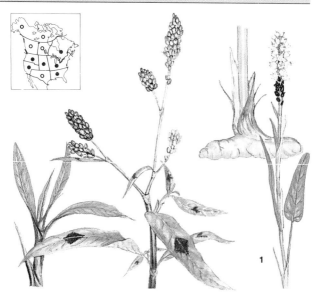

A spreading annual plant with smooth reddish stems; there is a swelling above each node which gives the stem a jointed appearance. The lance-shaped leaves have fringed leaf bases and often have black blotches. Tight spikes of pink, petal-less flowers are followed by spikes of shining brown fruits.

Found in waste places and cultivated ground, especially where the land is wet, where it may reach 24in tall. Throughout the USA and Canada.

The young leaves can be used in salads or cooked and served like spinach. The bulbils (small bulbs found on the lower parts of the flower stalks) of **Alpine Bistort** (1) can be eaten raw and the young roots of the same plant can be roasted or baked, like potatoes.

Alpine Bistort grows in alpine and arctic areas of Canada and northern USA. The leaves of many other related plants are also edible, although some of them are too peppery to taste good.

SHEEP SORREL

Harvest: SPRING TO FALL

An annual or perennial plant, with a clump of dark green arrow-shaped basal leaves and an erect, leafy flowering stem, up to 20in tall. Tiny green or reddish flowers grow in clusters in narrow elongated spikes and are followed by tiny, shiny brown, three-angled nutlets enclosed by calyces.

Found in disturbed ground, on roadsides and in gardens, in grassland and fields, usually in acid soils. Throughout much of the USA and Canada, except the far north and the south.

Gather basal leaves in spring and summer, but stem leaves may be tough. They can be used with other greens in salads, as a potherb or in soups. They can also be cooked with eggs and butter to make a sauce for use with fish. They should not be eaten in large quantities as they contain oxalic acid.

Sorrel is a similar plant found in Canada and northern USA, which can be used in the same ways. The many different kinds of docks are related and their leaves are also edible.

DANDELION

Harvest: FALL TO EARLY SUMMER

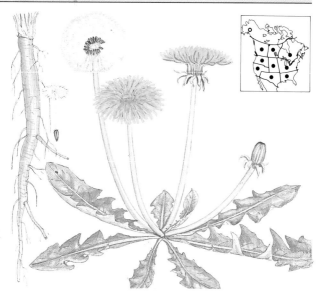

A small rosette-forming perennial plant with a long thin taproot and a clump of deep green leaves. The hollow flower stems exude a milky juice when broken. Bright yellow flower-heads grow singly on long stalks. Fruits are distinctive "clocks," round balls of parachuted seeds.

This is a familiar weed in lawns and gardens, on roadsides and waste ground throughout the USA and southern Canada. Introduced from Europe.

Young leaves and the blanched leaf bases can be used in salads or boiled as a green vegetable. Flowers can be used to make dandelion wine. Roots can be used in winter as a vegetable (peel and boil, serve with butter) or dried for two days and then roasted and ground to make dandelion coffee.

Young **Wild Lettuce** leaves can also be used in salads. **Chicory** leaves and the crown at the top of the root can be used in the same way. Its roots can be used as a coffee substitute.

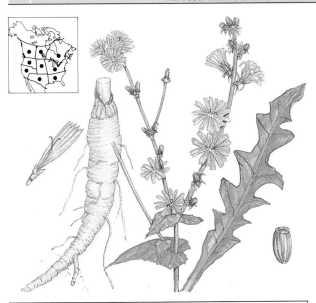

A perennial plant with a large taproot and a branched, erect stem up to 5ft tall. It has alternate, lance-shaped, toothed leaves and distinctive blue flower heads grow in the axils of the upper leaves. The fruits which follow are tiny nutlets.

Found along roadsides, in vacant lots, waste ground and fields throughout the USA and Canada. Introduced from Europe.

Use the leaves and the crown at the top of the root in very early spring as they soon become bitter. Cook and serve with butter as a green vegetable or use in salads. The roots may be dried and roasted, then ground for use as a coffee substitute.

Dandelion leaves and leaf bases can be used in the same way. Its roots can be used for making dandelion coffee.

PIGWEED
Harvest: SPRING TO WINTER

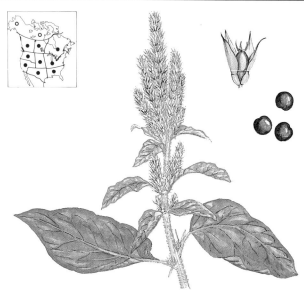

A large, coarse, annual plant, up to 6ft tall, with rough hairy stems and long, lance-shaped leaves. The green flowers grow in dense, branched terminal spikes and in long clusters in the leaf axils. Tiny black seeds grow in flattened fruits; the fruits are partly enclosed in pointed, rigid bracts.

Found growing as a weed in waste places, on roadsides and cultivated ground throughout the USA and Canada.

Young leaves can be used from spring plants, when they are only a few inches high, as a potherb or with other greens in a mixed salad. Dried leaves can be used in soups. Seeds should be gathered before they drop from the plant and eaten whole or ground into flour for use in muffins or pancakes.

Several other pigweeds grow in similar habitats. Their leaves and seeds can be used in the same way.

LAMB'S QUARTERS

Harvest: SPRING AND FALL

A large annual weed, up to 2ft tall, with reddish, mealy stems (covered with bladder-like hairs.) Lower leaves are broad and rhomboidal, upper ones lance-shaped; they are green above and mealy beneath. Small green flowers are borne in clusters in dense spikes. Brown seeds grow enclosed in persistent petals.

Found growing as a weed in waste places, on roadsides and cultivated ground, particularly where the soil is rich in nitrogen, throughout the USA and Canada.

Pick young shoots in spring or growing tips later. Boil or steam in a little water, like spinach (bulk greatly reduces in cooking,) or cook like asparagus. Add raw shoots to salads. Rich in vitamins A and C, protein and minerals. Grind seeds in fall and use as cereal or add to other flours for pancakes.

One of many widespread goosefoots and oraches, like the red-fruited Strawberry-blite, which can be used as potherbs. Some taste unpleasant, may be toxic and should be avoided.

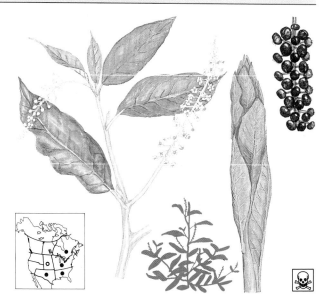

A leafy, hairless, clump-forming perennial plant, up to 9ft tall, with a disagreeable scent. It has several reddish, branched stems and many large, lance-shaped leaves. Long drooping sprays of white flowers are followed by drooping sprays of purple-black berries.

Found in waste places, on roadsides and on cultivated ground, in southern Canada and eastern and southern USA.

Harvest young shoots in spring, before they are 6in tall or leaves unfold. Boil them in two changes of water and then cook in fresh boiling water until tender. Serve like asparagus. Use only young shoots — the rest of the plant is poisonous. Do not use young shoots tinged with red as these are poisonous.

No similar edible plants.

FIREWEED

A perennial plant with widely spreading roots, from which grow erect leafy stems, up to 4ft tall. Narrow, dark green stem leaves grow angled upwards. Rosy purple flowers grow in large terminal flower spikes and are followed by erect seed capsules which split lengthwise to release many feathery seeds.

Often forms wide colonies in woodland clearings and on disturbed ground, especially after fire. Throughout the USA and Canada, in mountain areas in the south.

Gather young shoots in spring and cook like asparagus or make into soup. In summer, young leaves and flower buds can be added to salads. Young leaves can also be cooked as a vegetable like spinach. Older leaves can be dried and used to make tea. Not the most tasty wild plant but very common.

River Beauty, a willowherb from Canada, northeastern and western USA, has much better flavored young spring shoots. Other willowherbs can also be used in the same ways.

ASPARAGUS
Harvest: SPRING

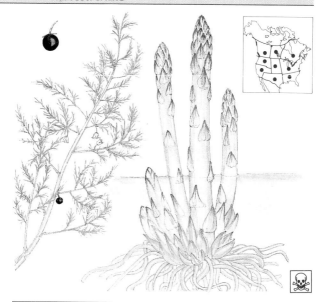

A perennial plant with thick underground stems from which grow many erect shoots. In spring these are pale and fleshy, but they grow 6ft tall, branched and feathery in summer with many scale-like leaves. The flowers are yellow-green bells hanging from the upper stems. Fruits are globular red berries.

Found in sandy well-drained soils, in fields, on roadsides and disturbed ground. A garden escape, introduced from Europe.

Use only the young stalks, like the cultivated asparagus: older stalks are toxic. Wash and tie stalks into a bundle. Steam in boiling water for about 15 minutes and serve with butter. Use also for soups and in any asparagus recipes.

No similar species.

OSTRICH FERN

Harvest: SPRING

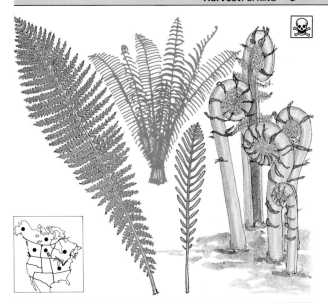

A large fern which forms vase-like clumps. The arching, plume-like, dark green outer fronds are sterile while the inner, smaller, stiff brown central fronds are fertile. Coiled edible fiddleheads (young fronds) emerge amongst last year's fertile fronds in spring; they are covered in papery brown scales.

Found besides streams and ponds, in swamps and moist forests, in bottomlands. Southern Canada and south in eastern USA to Missouri.

Gather fiddleheads in spring when they are less than 6in tall and scrape off the inedible papery brown scales. They can be used raw in salads or cooked like asparagus.

Bracken fiddleheads are often recommended for eating but they are poisonous raw. It has been suggested that they can cause stomach cancer even when cooked, so are probably best avoided.

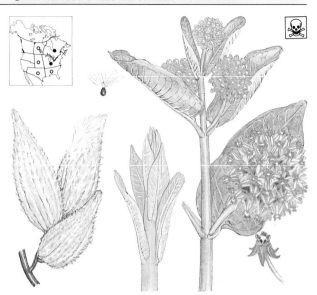

A perennial plant with upright downy stems, up to 6ft tall. The opposite leaves are thick and leathery, with wavy margins, hairy upper surfaces and milky sap. Flowers have five reflexed petals; they may be dull rose, purple or greenish white and grow in dense heads. Fruits are clusters of warty green pods.

Found in dry soils, on roadsides and woodland margins, in fields and meadows. Northeastern USA and into southern Canada, south to Kansas in the mountains and west into the prairies.

New shoots can be used when less than 8in tall, leaves picked when just opened and clusters of flowers and buds used when young. Cook in several quick changes of boiling water to remove slightly toxic sap, and simmer until tender. Serve as a vegetable. Treated pods may be used like okra in soup.

Showy Milkweed (a western species with pinkish flowers and velvety leaves) is also edible but many milkweeds are poisonous. The poisonous Dogbane has milky sap but is hairless.

Large annual plant, up to 4ft tall, with a branched erect stem and alternate leaves. The lower leaves are lobed, the upper ones narrow with wavy margins. The flowers are yellow, in long elongating sprays terminating the stems. They are followed by long green pod-like fruits which contain many small seeds.

Found in waste ground, yards, on roadsides and in fields throughout much of the USA and Canada. A weed introduced from Europe.

In early spring, pick the very young outer leaves — new ones will then grow. In later spring leaves become bitter but can be blanched on the plant. Use the leaves as a green vegetable or in salads. Pick buds and flowers when they appear and use like broccoli. Seeds can be ground to make mustard.

Winter Cress can be used in a similar way. It grows in wet places and is similar in appearance to mustard, differing in details of leaves, flowers and fruits.

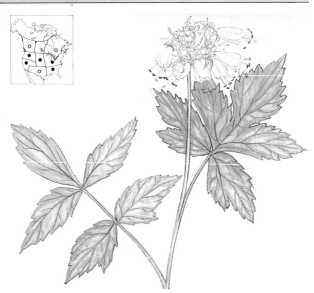

Perennial plants with a rosette of leaves and erect flowering stems, up to 3ft tall. The toothed leaves may be lobed or compound and often look stained, as if with water. The white or lilac flowers grow in clusters on long stalks in the leaf axils; the stamens of each flower project beyond the petals.

There are several species of waterleaf found throughout the USA. They grow in moist rich woods, in damp clearings and beside streams.

The leaves from the basal rosettes of waterleafs may be gathered in spring, before the flowers appear. They make an excellent cooked green vegetable.

The different species of waterleafs vary mostly in the shape of their leaves and in flower color; they can all be used in the same way.

A large woolly plant, up to 6ft tall, with a rank scent and thick, hollow, ridged stems. The leaves have swollen stalks, three maple-like leaflets and may measure up to 3ft across. White, sometimes purple-tinged flowers are borne in large, compound umbels and are followed by flattened winged fruits.

Found in damp ground in woods and thickets throughout Canada and much of the USA, in mountains in the south and absent from the southwestern deserts.

Gather the young leaves and shoots in spring, before the leaves are fully unfurled, wash and cook in several changes of water; they resemble cooked celery. Young roots can be used like parsnips. Seeds can be dried and used as a seasoning.

Edible Wild Carrot has one purple flower in each umbel. These plants must be identified carefully, as related plants, like Water Hemlock which has red-streaked stems, are poisonous.

STINGING NETTLE

Harvest: SPRING TO SUMMER

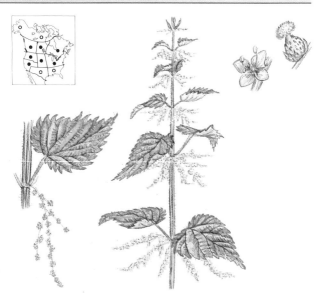

A large perennial plant, with a clump of four-angled stems up to 3ft high, bearing pairs of roughly toothed, deep green pointed leaves. The whole plant is clothed with stinging hairs. The small green, petal-less flowers grow in "tassels" in the leaf axils, male and female on separate plants.

Found in woods, waste places, on roadsides and on cultivated land in eastern and central USA and in most of Canada, except the far north. Introduced from Europe.

Wear gloves when picking to avoid the stinging hairs. Pick tender green shoots in spring or young leaves at the tops of summer stems. Simmer in a little water (boiling destroys hairs) and serve with butter and seasonings. Nettles can also be used to make tea or beer. They are rich in vitamins.

Wood Nettle and Slender Nettle are similar plants, both found in the east. They can be used in the same ways but must be handled with gloves.

MALLOWS

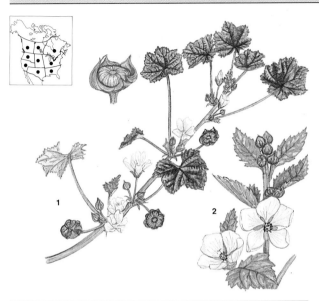

Mallows are mucilaginous, annual or perennial, hairy plants. They have a large taproot and large, palmately lobed, alternately arranged leaves. Showy white or pink flowers grow singly or in small clusters in the leaf axils. Fruits resemble segmented cheeses enclosed in a persistent calyx.

Found in waste places and cultivated ground, on roadsides and in farm yards throughout the USA and southern Canada. Marsh Mallow grows beside brackish marshes on the eastern coast.

Use young leaves as a potherb or to thicken soups, like okra. Unripe green fruits can be added to salads. The roots of Marsh Mallow can be boiled until thick and made into marshmallows, and the stock from boiling roots or leaves can be used as a substitute for egg white in meringue. Its buds can be pickled.

Common Mallow (1) is the most widespread; it is a sprawling annual weed. Musk Mallow has divided leaves and purple flowers. **Marsh Mallow (2)** is a stout plant with pink flowers.

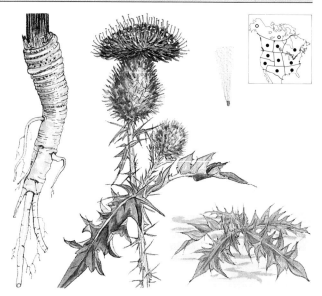

Spiny annual, biennial or perennial plants with erect stems, up to 4ft tall; and deeply toothed or divided, spine-tipped leaves. Some have spiny stems, others have spineless stems. Flower heads are composed of a rounded bristly "base" and a dense cluster of red-purple florets. Seeds have many hairs.

Found on roadsides and in waste places, in fields and pastures throughout the USA and Canada. Some of the most common are introduced from Europe.

Remove spines from young leaves and add raw to salads or cook as a green vegetable. Young stems can be peeled and eaten raw or cooked. Roots from first year plants of biennial thistles (like Bull Thistle, illustrated) can also be peeled, then boiled and fried; or they can be cooked and ground into flour.

There are many species of thistles, some of them better to eat than others. **Bull Thistle** (illustrated) is one of the most common and most useful.

An annual plant, up to 20in tall, with an erect prickly stem. The leaves are lance-shaped, often with clasping bases and with prickly, lobed edges and prickles on the main veins of the undersides. Leaves and stem are filled with milky juice. Clusters of yellow flower heads grow on the branched stem.

Found on vacant lots and roadsides, disturbed ground and waste places, also on walls and stony ground. Throughout southern Canada and the USA. A weed introduced from Europe.

Only the young leaves are tender enough to eat. Gather them in spring before the plants grow to 10in tall. Very young leaves may be used raw in salads, older ones cooked in a little water and used as a green vegetable. The leaves have a bitter flavor. Flower heads may be used in casseroles.

The leaves of other Wild Lettuces and of Blue Lettuces can be used in the same way.

CLEAVERS

Harvest: SPRING AND SUMMER

A scrambling annual plant, up to 4ft tall; its lax stems have hooked bristles in four rows. The linear leaves are also bristly and grow in whorls of six or eight. Tiny white flowers are borne in the axils of the upper leaves and are followed by small, rounded, bristly fruits which grow in pairs.

Found in thickets, moist shady woodland and waste places throughout the USA and Canada, except the extreme north.

Steam or boil the young spring growths and serve with butter and seasoning. Cooked shoots can also be used cold in salads with asparagus. In summer, the tiny bristly fruits make an excellent coffee substitute — slow roast them till brown, grind and simmer in water. Strain before serving.

Cleavers is one of a group of plants called bedstraws. Their young shoots can all be used in the same way, but many are very small.

A perennial vine with tough, green, branching stems, often with scattered thorns, and alternately arranged, leathery, triangular leaves. It clings by means of tendrils in the leaf axils. Greenish male or female flowers are borne in clusters on long stalks and are followed by globular black berries.

Found in open woods, on roadsides, on disturbed ground and in old fields, in eastern and midwestern USA.

Young crisp shoots, leaves and tendrils can be eaten raw as a trail nibble or in salads. Older shoots can be boiled and eaten like asparagus or allowed to cool and used as a salad. The tuberous roots can be pounded to obtain a gelatinous sediment which can be used to thicken stews or jelly.

Greenbriar (a more thorny plant with round shiny leaves) and Carrion Flower (a thornless plant with heart-shaped leaves) are similar. Their young shoots can be used in the same way.

59

GLASSWORT

Harvest: SPRING TO FALL

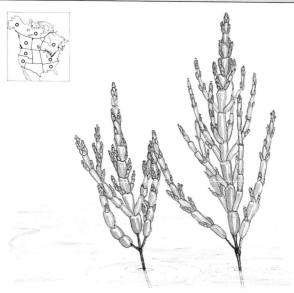

An often sprawling, succulent, annual plant, with many stiff, jointed, red-tinged green stems, growing up to 16in high. The leaves are so minute and scale-like that the plant appears leafless. Tiny flowers grow in crowded spikes at the tips of upright branches.

Found in salt marshes, on beaches and mudflats along both the Atlantic and Pacific coasts. Also on alkaline soils inland in northern USA and Canada.

The growing tips of the stems are tender and salty and good as a trail nibble. They can also be served in salads with other salad greens or potatoes, or boiled and eaten with butter as a vegetable. Glasswort pickles are traditional pickles made with young tips.

Several other species of glassworts are found in similar habitats. They are difficult to distinguish from each other and all are edible.

SPEARMINT

Harvest: SUMMER

A perennial creeping plant, with many erect four-angled stems up to 3ft tall. The leaves are broadly lance-shaped, toothed and scented and they grow in opposite pairs. Tiny light mauve flowers are borne in dense whorls in upper leaf axils. Fruits are tiny nutlets, borne in fours in the persistent calyxes.

Found in wet and damp places along roadsides, beside streams and ditches. Introduced from Europe, widely cultivated and extensively naturalized in the wild.

The young leaves at the tops of the stems are the best. Regular picking encourages new young side growths. Fresh leaves can be chopped into salads or used to make mint jelly. Fresh leaves can be added to chinese tea to add a mint flavor or dried leaves can be steeped in boiling water to make tea.

Peppermint has a peppermint scent to its leaves. Its leaves can be used to make candy or infused to make tea. Other mint species can be used in similar ways.

A perennial plant, with erect, leafy, four-angled stems up to 3ft tall and opposite, pointed-oval or long-triangular, toothed leaves. The showy two-lipped flowers grow in terminal heads surrounded by bracts; the bracts are often tinged with lilac.

Found in dry thickets, woodland edges and clearings. Throughout the USA except Calif., and in southern Canada except the east coast; mostly in uplands in the south.

The leaves are most well-known for their use as a tea, or as a flavoring added to other teas. They may be used fresh or dried. The flowers may also be added to the tea. The entire plant can also be used as a potherb.

Bee-balm or Oswego Tea is a related plant with bright red flowers; it grows beside streams and in moist woods in eastern USA and Canada. Its leaves are also used to make tea.

WINTERGREEN

Harvest: ALL YEAR

A creeping, low-growing, evergreen plant with erect stems, up to 8in high, and oval, shiny, leathery leaves that smell of wintergreen when crushed. The waxy white, urn-shaped flowers are usually solitary and borne on drooping stalks beneath the leaves. Fruits are rounded, bright red berries.

Grows on poor acid soils in woodland clearings, in deciduous and coniferous woods. Eastern Canada to the Great Lakes and Minnesota and south to Georgia.

The leaves can be picked throughout the year and used to make tea; cover the leaves in boiling water and leave for a day. Reheat before drinking. Fruits are best eaten after frost, either raw or in pancakes and muffins. The plant contains an aspirin-like substance which reduces fever.

Snowberry (1), from Canadian coniferous forests, has bright green leaves. It is related to Wintergreen and its leaves can be used for tea or as a vegetable; its fruits make good jam.

A low-growing evergreen shrub, up to 3ft tall with densely hairy, red-brown twigs. The dark green, oblong leaves have inrolled margins; the lower surface of the leaf is densely hairy with white hairs, turning rusty as they age. Terminal clusters of white flowers are followed by dry capsules.

Found in mountain woods, heaths, fens and cold bogs in Canada and northern and western USA.

The leaves may be gathered to make tea at any time of year, but winter leaves are not as good. Pick the leaves with rust-colored hairs and dry in sun or in an oven. Steep the leaves in boiling water for 10 minutes to make a pleasant tea, but do not boil them as boiling may release a harmful alkaloid.

The leaves of Northern Labrador Tea may also be used to make tea. Mountain Labrador Tea, found in the Pacific areas of Canada and the USA, is said to be poisonous.

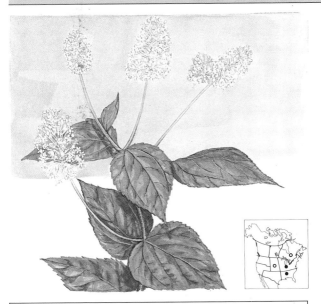

A low bushy shrub, up to 4ft tall. It has thin, densely hairy, red-brown twigs and alternately arranged, deciduous leaves. The leaves are simple with fine teeth on the edges and three prominent ribs. Tiny white flowers grow in dense cylindrical clusters in the leaf axils.

Found in open woods and roadsides, in prairies, in well-drained coarse soils. Eastern USA, west to Kansas and north into the prairies and eastern Canada.

Gather leaves (especially while the bushes are in flower) in dry weather in summer, and dry them thoroughly, in an oven or in the sun. Use them to make an excellent caffeine-free tea. The bark of the roots can be dried and used as a sedative.

Many species of Californian lilacs, of which New Jersey Tea is one, grow in the USA, especially in Calif. Their leaves can be used for tea, although some species are better than others.

🌼 BUDS & FLOWERS

Not many plants are used primarily for their buds or flowers. However, many of the plants that have edible leaves or roots, also have edible flowers. They may be used as a vegetable like broccoli (which is actually a cluster of flower buds), included in salads or made into fritters. Other flowers can be used to make drinks and wine; these are often rich in nectar and scent and give the wine a distinctive bouquet.

Most of the plants with edible flowers in this book have been included in other sections, since their flowers are of lesser importance. They include:

Small, usually perennial plants either with several branched stems or with leaves and flowers growing from a single crown. The leaves may be rounded, divided or lobed. The blue-violet, white or yellow flowers grow on long stalks; each has five petals and a spur at the back.

There are very many violets in N. America, both rare and common, mostly growing in damp places, in woods and meadows. In the south they are most common in mountain areas.

Use violets only when they are abundant and you are sure that this is not a rare one. The flowers can be candied — dip in a mixture of egg-white and rose water and then into sugar, leave overnight. Use the leaves in a green salad or cook and serve like spinach. Use dried leaves to make tea.

It is best to use violet leaves only when the plants are in flower and you can be sure of identifying them accurately, since their leaves may resemble other, possibly toxic, plants.

In botanical terms, the fruits of a plant are the structures which contain the seeds. These fruits may be small or large, fleshy, sweet & juicy, dry & hard, covered with hooks, or fly with a parachute. In more general usage, the word "fruit" is restricted to sweet & juicy or fleshy fruits, & in this section only plants with these kinds of fruits have been included.

The fruits are most common in late summer & fall; they are often rich in sugars & vitamins & are attractive to birds, insects & other animals. They may be difficult to gather if high on a tree or deep in a bramble patch. They may be eaten raw, used to make sauces, jams & jellies, baked into pies or used in muffins & pancakes. Many can also be crushed to make drinks or fermented to make wines.

As well as the plants in this section, plants with other kinds of edible fruits are on the following pages:

Common Milkweed (p. 50)
Cleavers (p. 58)
Wintergreen (p. 63)
Honey Mesquite (p. 115)
Prickly Pear (p. 116)
Spicebush (p. 118)
Junipers (p. 119)

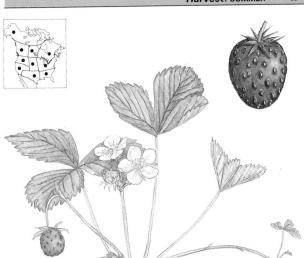

Forms small perennial clumps of hairy, compound leaves. Each leaf has three toothed leaflets. Flowers white with five petals and five sepals, borne in small clusters on long stalks. Fruits are small strawberries.

Found in open woods, on woodland edges and in grassland throughout the USA and southern Canada, but more common at high altitudes in the south.

Wild strawberries are small and sweet. Eat fresh, with cream and sugar or use in any strawberry recipe. Steep fresh or dried leaves in boiling water for 5 minutes for a drink rich in Vitamin C.

Wood Strawberry bears similar fruits; it grows in moist rocky woods throughout the USA and Canada, except the far north.

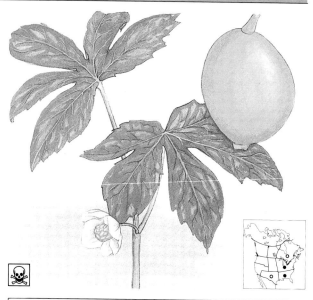

A perennial plant which forms dense patches of upright stems, up to 18in tall, each with one or two very large, deeply divided, umbrella-like leaves. A leaf may measure up to 14in across. Stems with two leaves bear a single nodding, white waxy flower which is followed by an egg-shaped yellow berry.

Found in rich moist deciduous woods and on shady roadsides, in clearings and meadows. Eastern USA and Canada, reaching southern Quebec in the north and Texas in the south.

Only the pulp from ripe May Apples is edible; unripe fruits, seeds and all other parts of the plant are poisonous. Gather the yellow fruits when the leaves are withering and turning yellow. Remove seeds and eat the pulp raw or use to make jams and pie fillings. The juice can also be added to lemonade.

No other similar species.

GROUND CHERRIES

Harvest: SUMMER

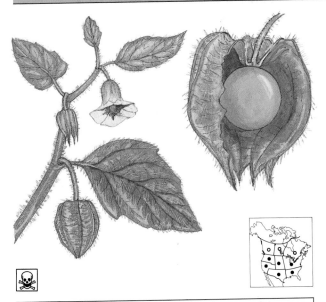

Coarse annual plants, up to 2ft tall, with weak stems and alternate leaves. The leaves are large, pointed and hairy. The trumpet-shaped flowers grow in the axils of upper leaves; they are yellow, often with a dark center. Ripe fruits vary from yellow to purple; they are enclosed in a lantern-like calyx.

Found in open woods, fields, waste places and on roadsides throughout much of the USA and Canada.

Use only ripe berries, which often ripen on the ground in their lanterns after falling from the plant. Their presence on the ground is not a guarantee of their ripeness. Unripe berries and leaves are poisonous. Ripe berries may be eaten raw, used in pies, jams or preserves.

There are many species of ground cherries, with fruits varying in color from yellow to red or purple. All have the distinctive lanterns around the fruits.

WILD GRAPES

Harvest: SPRING AND LATE SUMMER TO FALL

Perennial climbing vines, with tough branched stems and large lobed leaves. They cling by means of branched tendrils growing in the leaf axils. The small greenish flowers form elongated clusters and are followed by purple or black grapes. These may have a whitish bloom and contain several pear-shaped seeds.

Found along woodland edges and in thickets. There are many species of wild grapes which grow throughout the USA and southern Canada.

Harvest grapes in late summer or fall, depending on species and area. Many are too acid to eat raw but can be cooked in pies. Grape juice can be obtained by crushing the berries and used for wine or jelly. Use the young leaves in spring as a green vegetable or in any stuffed vine leaf recipe.

Moonseed is a twisting vine that has black poisonous berries. It can be distinguished from grapes by its lack of tendrils and the single crescent-shaped seed in each berry.

Shrubs up to 10ft tall, with arching spiny or thorny branches and alternate compound leaves. The leaves have between three and nine leaflets, depending on species. Flowers are large and conspicuous, pink or rose-colored, with five petals and many stamens. Fruits are smooth, fleshy red hips.

Found in open woods and woodland edges, in hedgerows and old pastures, on roadsides, dunes and along rivers. About 35 species distributed throughout USA and Canada.

Rose hips are rich in Vitamin C. Pick them after frost and make rosehip syrup by boiling them with sugar and water and straining the juice; it can be used as a vitamin supplement for children or as a sauce for icecream. Hips can also be made into jellies or dried. Rose tea is made by infusing leaves.

Sweetbriar (illustrated) is a widely naturalized European wild rose. It has elongated hips. Carolina Rose grows in the east; it has globular hips. California Rose has egg-shaped hips.

Upright or trailing, prickly shrubs, up to 10ft tall, with arching green stems and dark green, compound leaves. The leaves usually have five rounded leaflets. Clusters of white flowers are followed by sweet, juicy black fruits. A fruit consists of many sections, each containing one seed.

Found in woods and along woodland edges, in hedgerows, along roadsides and on disturbed ground. Northeastern USA, west into Minnesota and south to Tennessee.

Harvest berries when ripe and eat fresh with cream and sugar; eat with pancakes or make into jam, jelly or wine. Use in many berry recipes or mix with apples to make blackberry and apple pie. Dried leaves can be steeped in boiling water to make tea.

Raspberries have three to seven leaflets and red or black fruits. The related Thimbleberry is a western plant with spineless stems, five-lobed leaves and bright red fruits.

Spreading or trailing, prickly shrub, up to 6ft tall, with stiff hairs on the often white-powdered stems. The compound leaves have three to seven leaflets, pale green to whitish and hairy on the underside. Small clusters of whitish flowers are followed by bright red, many-sectioned, globular fruits.

Found on woodland margins and in clearings, on roadsides and in old fields across southern Canada, into northeastern USA and south through the Rocky Mountains.

Harvest berries when ripe and eat fresh with cream and sugar; eat with pancakes or make into jam, jelly or wine. Use them in any berry recipe. Dried leaves can be steeped in boiling water to make tea.

Black Raspberry grows in northeastern and north central USA; its leaves have three to five leaflets and it has purple to black fruits. **Blackberry** has five leaflets and black fruits.

CURRANTS
Harvest: SUMMER

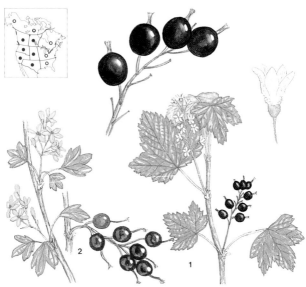

Small upright or trailing shrubs, some with spines on their branches, and with alternate, maple-like leaves. The white, pink, yellow or greenish flowers grow in drooping sprays and are followed by berries — currants. These may be red, black or bluish in color and are often juicy; each has several seeds.

Found mostly in damp woods, swamps, shady streambanks, others in drier areas. Most grow in midwestern and western USA and Canada, some also grow in the east.

Red and black currants are the sweetest and most juicy, bluish ones are often less good. They are used to make jellies and jams, fruit juices and pies. They may also be added to fruit salads or combined with dough to make muffins. Dried and mixed with meat and sugar they are used to make pemmican.

Wild Red and **Black Currants** (1) are found across the continent. **Golden Currant** (2) grows in the midwest and western USA and Canada; it has golden flowers and red fruits.

GOOSEBERRIES

Harvest: SUMMER

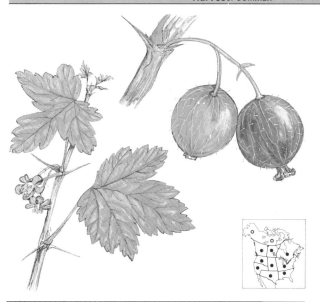

Small upright or arching shrubs, with bristly, spiny branches, and alternate, maple-like leaves. Small reddish flowers grow singly or in small clusters. Fruits are gooseberries — large translucent, smooth or bristly berries, red or purple in color, and with the remains of the flower hanging beneath.

Several species found in many different habitats, from moist woods to rocky uplands and open slopes. Throughout much of Canada and the USA, more common in the west.

Smooth gooseberries can be eaten raw, but bristly berries are best cooked, when the hairs are softened. They tend to be quite tart and should only be picked when fully ripe. Gooseberries can be used in jams and jellies, in pies and fruit sauces.

There are several species of gooseberries, with smooth or bristly fruits and varying in distribution. They are all edible. Bristly Black Currant also has bristly fruits.

SPANISH BAYONET

Harvest: SPRING AND SUMMER

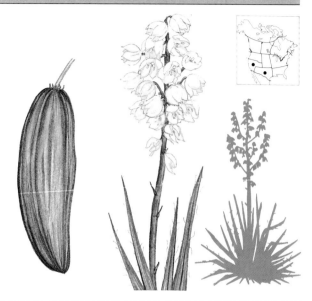

A large perennial plant with rosettes of stiff, sharply pointed, slightly rolled, linear leaves, up to 4ft tall. The leaves have fibrous margins. The flowers are borne in upright flower spikes; they are like drooping bells, waxy white or greenish. Fruits are fleshy capsules, red-brown when ripe.

Found in sandy or rocky soils, on hillsides, in grasslands and deserts. Southwestern USA, from southern California to Texas and Mexico, north to Utah and Colorado.

Ripe fruits can be eaten raw, or they may be halved, the fiber and seeds scraped out, and then roasted. Fruit pulp can be used in pies. Young flower stalks can be roasted and the core eaten with butter. Young flower stalks and buds can also be boiled, chopped and used in salads.

Other yuccas, like Blue Yucca of the prairies and Bear-grass of the southeast, have flowers and buds that can be used in the same way. Some have fleshy fruits, others have dry fruits.

COMMON BARBERRY

Harvest: FALL

A medium-sized shrub, up to 10ft tall, with many tripartite spines on the yellowish branches. The deciduous, oval, finely toothed leaves grow crowded together on short shoots. Clusters of yellow flowers are followed by drooping clusters of orange-red, oblong berries in late summer and fall.

Introduced from Europe, this shrub is widely planted in northeastern USA, where it has become naturalized in fence rows and on roadsides, in waste ground and disturbed woods.

Ripe berries can be used for jelly, by themselves or with other fruits where a tart fruit or pectin is needed. They can also be used in recipes calling for cooked fruits or made into an excellent cold drink.

Other barberry species grow in other parts of the USA and in southern Canada. Their berries can be used in the same ways.

J ☕

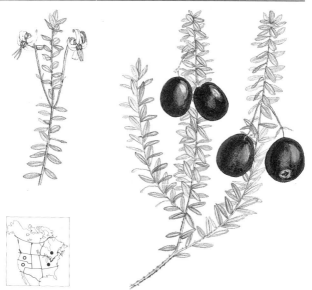

A low trailing shrub with slender brown stems and small, alternate, leathery evergreen leaves. The pink flowers grow singly or in small clusters on long stalks in the axils of the leaves; each has four backwardly pointing petals. Fruits are globular berries, green at first, turning red when ripe.

Found in acid soils, in open bogs and swamps, and along the shores of acid lakes in the east, from Newfoundland and Nova Scotia south to Minnesota and North Carolina.

These wild cranberries can be used in a fruit sauce to accompany turkey, like the cultivated ones. Boil in a little water until the berries burst, then simmer and add sugar. They can also be frozen, dried or made into preserves.

The Small Cranberry is found in the same range as the Cranberry. Mountain Cranberries are widespread throughout Canada. Both these plants also have edible berries.

J

BLUEBERRY

Harvest: SUMMER

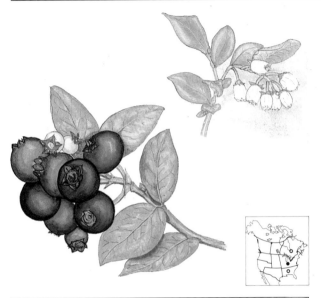

A tall, much branched shrub, up to 12ft high, with alternate, yellow-green, deciduous leaves. The pinkish, urn-shaped flowers are produced in dense terminal clusters on the twigs. The fruits are fleshy, globular blue-black berries, with a whitish bloom.

Found in wet woods, swamps and bogs in lowlands, occasionally in drier upland woods, always growing in acid soils. Eastern Canada, southwards to Wisconsin and Georgia.

Pick and use the berries as a trail snack or in a variety of berry recipes. They can be used in pies, jams and preserves, made into blueberry muffins or bannocks, mixed with other fruits in summer pudding, or used in fritters. They can also be dried for storage.

Late Sweet Blueberries and Huckleberries grow on low thicket-forming plants; the berries are similar. Bilberry is another related, low-growing plant with juicy berries.

HIGHBUSH CRANBERRY
Harvest: FALL AND WINTER

An upright shrub, up to 5ft tall, with opposite, deciduous, three-lobed leaves which are hairy beneath. Dense clusters of flowers have showy white ones around edges and small ones in the center. Fruits are bright red, juicy, translucent berries, each containing a single flattened stone.

Found in wet thickets and woods, on rocky slopes and along the edges of streams. Northern USA and southern Canada, from coast to coast.

Berries may be gathered once they ripen in summer but they are tart at this stage and become sweeter after frost; they are best picked through fall and winter. They can be used to make a sauce like cranberry sauce, providing the stones are removed. They can also be made into juice or jelly.

Cranberries are unrelated creeping plants. Highbush Cranberry is more closely related to Squashberry, whose fruits can be used in the same way.

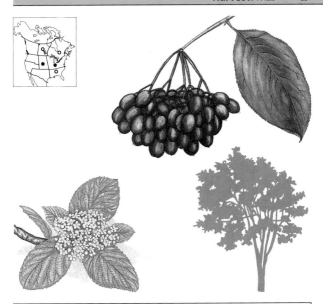

A small tree or large shrub, up to 30ft tall, with opposite, deciduous, oval-pointed leaves which have fine-toothed margins. Dense heads of white flowers are followed by clusters of sweet, juicy, blue-black berries. Each has a single flattened seed.

Found along the edges of streams and in marshes, on rocky slopes, in wet woods and on woodland margins. Northeastern USA, west to Minnesota and north into southern Canada.

Berries can be picked in fall and eaten raw but the seeds must be removed. They are also good for use in pies, fruit sauces and jellies. The fruits must be pulped, strained to remove seeds, and then added to other, usually tart fruits.

Hobblebush, found in northern USA east of the Great Lakes, is a related plant with fruits which can be used in the same way. It is a straggling shrub with clusters of black fruits.

SILVER BUFFALOBERRY

Harvest: SUMMER AND FALL

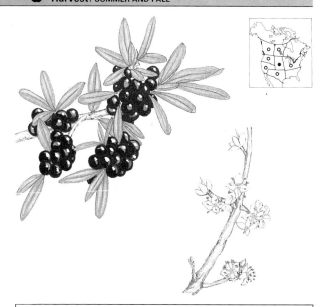

A small tree or spreading shrub, up to 15ft tall, with thorny branches, covered with silvery scales. The deciduous leaves are opposite and leathery with dense silver scales. Small male and female flowers grow on separate trees and female flowers are followed by many bright red, fleshy berries.

Found on streambanks and in low-lying meadows, from Manitoba to Alberta and southwards to Kansas and New Mexico.

Gather berries in summer and use for jelly, mash and strain for a pleasant tart drink, cook with meat or make into a sauce like cranberry sauce, by pureeing the fruit. Berries become sweeter after frost and are good raw or with sugar. They may be dried in the sun for storage.

Canada Buffaloberry grows throughout Canada and the USA, except the southeast and Calif. It is a smaller shrub with bitter berries that are edible if cooked with sugar.

COMMON ELDER

Harvest: SPRING AND SUMMER

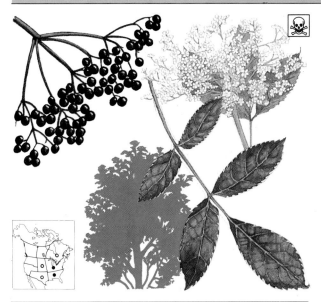

A broad shrub, up to 12ft tall, with soft, pithy, spreading branches. The dark green leaves are opposite and compound, with 5–11 leaflets each. The white scented flowers grow in flat clusters and are followed by large, flat clusters of small, black, juicy berries.

Found in damp rich soils, along woodland margins and in thickets, beside trails and streams, along fences and ditches in the USA east of the Rockies and in southeastern Canada.

Harvest flower clusters on a sunny day in late spring to make fritters. The flowers can be soaked with lemons in water to make elderflower lemonade or made into wine or champagne. The fruits can be used with apples and plums to make pies and jams or made into elderberry wine. Berries are rich in Vitamin C.

Unripe berries, shoots and leaves may be somewhat toxic. Some of the other elders have similar edible berries, but others may be bitter. Red Elder berries are toxic.

SMOOTH SUMAC
Harvest: SUMMER AND FALL

A small tree or large shrub, up to 20ft tall, with a few stout branches. It has large, deciduous, compound leaves with 11–31 saw-toothed, hairless leaflets. Dense cone-shaped clusters of whitish male and female flowers grow on separate plants. Fruits are dark red, fuzzy berries in similar dense clusters.

Found along roadsides and in waste land, abandoned fields and grasslands, woodland margins and clearings. Eastern USA, into southern Canada and west to the prairies. Also in the Rockies.

Suck raw berries when they have a glazed appearance, for lemony thirst-quenching taste. Fruits can be steeped in water for 15 minutes, then strained for a delicious drink; they can also be used to make jelly or syrup. They should be consumed in moderation as some people show an allergic reaction.

Staghorn Sumac and Squawbush berries can be used in the same way; the former has similar leaves, Squawbush three-lobed leaves. Avoid white-berried sumac as it is poisonous.

DOWNY SERVICEBERRY

Harvest: SUMMER

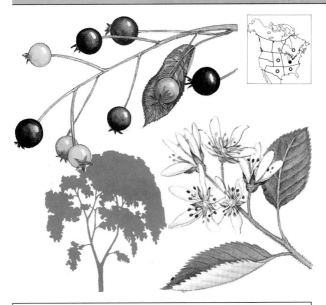

A small tree or large shrub, up to 40ft tall. The elliptical leaves have soft hairs on the underside when young and saw teeth on the margins. White star-like flowers appear before the leaves; each has five narrow petals. They are followed by clusters of rounded, dark red-purple, fleshy fruits.

Found in mixed deciduous woods, on rocky slopes and in valleys; also planted as an ornamental. Eastern USA except the southeast; also across the border into eastern Canada.

Fruits ripen in mid to late summer. Eat them raw or use in jams and jellies. They can also be used in pies and muffins or made into a fruit sauce. The fruits can be dried and stored like raisins or used to make pemmican.

Several other serviceberries, with similar fruits, occur in N. America. Western Serviceberry is the most widely distributed, common in the north and west; it has very dark fruits.

A deciduous tree or shrub, up to 40ft tall. Its compound leaves have 11–17 narrow, long-pointed, toothed leaflets. It has small white flowers growing in large flat-topped clusters, followed by similar clusters of red berries.

There are several species of Mountain Ashes found in woodland throughout Canada and the USA. Also, the European Mountain Ash or Rowan is often planted in streets and widely naturalized.

The ripe berries can be cooked after they have been exposed to frost or frozen. They can be made into jams or jellies, cooked into a fruit sauce like cranberries, or used in pies. They can also be made into wine. Berries can also be stored if kept in a dry place.

Northern Mountain Ash is illustrated. American Mountain Ash, from northeastern USA and Canada, has narrower leaflets; both have sticky buds. European Mountain Ash has woolly buds.

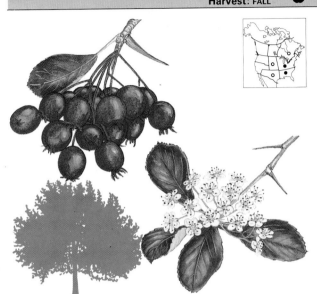

A small tree, up to 25ft tall, with a round spreading crown and dark gray branches armed with slender sharp spines. The deciduous leaves are simple, toothed and glossy dark green. Clusters of white or red five-petalled flowers are followed by dry, globular, dull green or red berries.

Found on hillsides and mountain slopes, in valleys and in old fields, throughout most of eastern USA except the far north. Also planted as a hedge and ornamental tree.

The fruits are best used to make jam or jelly; some may be sweet enough to eat raw. They may also be used to make tea, steeped in boiling water with mint leaves. Fruits can be dried for use later, or used to make pemmican.

One of many native hawthorns with similar fruits, all of which can be used in the same way, although some are sweeter than others. Most have fruits which ripen in the fall.

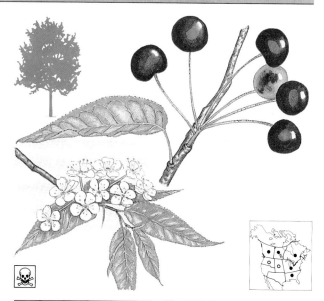

A small tree or large shrub, up to 30ft tall, with a narrow crown and red-brown bark. It has long, finely saw-toothed, shiny green leaves and clusters of white flowers on long stalks, appearing with the leaves in spring. Fruits are very small red cherries, growing in clusters, each with one stone.

Moist open woods and thickets, clearings; often most common amongst new growth in burnt areas. Northeastern USA from Maine to the Dakotas and across much of southern Canada.

Ripe fruits can be used to make jelly. Leaves and stones contain cyanide and should not be eaten.

Sour Cherry is naturalized in Canada, east and west USA; it has large, red, sour cherries. Sweet Cherry is cultivated; it has large red or purple cherries.

J

BLACK CHERRY

Harvest: SUMMER

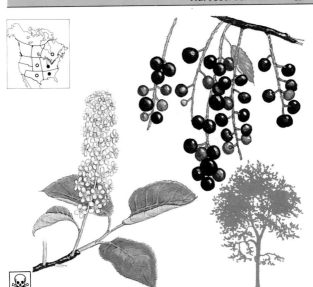

A medium-sized tree, up to 70ft tall, with gray bark fissured to expose inner reddish bark. The alternate leaves are shiny dark green, elliptical with saw-toothed margins. White flowers are borne in dense drooping spikes. Fruits are strings of small, juicy cherries, dark red turning black.

Found in woods and thickets throughout most of eastern USA.

The cherries are slightly bitter but can be eaten raw or with cream and sugar. They can also be used with apples to make fruit juice and jellies, or for muffins and pies, preserves and wine. Leaves and stones contain cyanide and should not be eaten.

Common Chokecherry occurs across northern USA and Canada; its dark red or black fruits can be used in the same way.

AMERICAN PLUM

Harvest: SUMMER

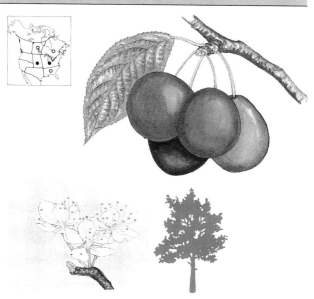

A small tree or thicket-forming shrub, up to 30ft tall, with alternate, dull green, elliptical, saw-toothed leaves. The short twigs end in spines. Small clusters of white five-petalled flowers appear before the leaves. The fruits are red or orange rounded plums, borne singly or in small clusters.

Found in mixed deciduous woods, along valleys and streams, fences and fields. From northeastern USA, south of the Great Lakes, west to the Dakotas and south to Alabama.

Ripe plums are sweet and may be eaten raw or used in any cultivated plum recipe. They are good for making jams and jellies; combine with sweeter fruits, like peaches, in pies or with strawberries in fruit compotes.

Other plums include Chickasaw Plum from the south, with red or yellow plums; Mexican Plum from the prairies, purple-red plums; Canada Plum from southern Canada, yellow-red plums.

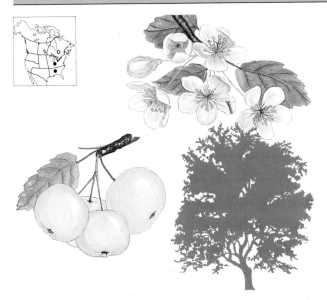

A small tree, up to 30ft tall, with fissured red-brown bark. Toothed, ovate, deciduous leaves grow with the flowers and apples on short side twigs. The clusters of fragrant white or pink, five-petalled flowers are followed by rather sour, yellow-green apples, growing on long stalks.

Found in forest clearings and margins, in old fields and beside streams. Varieties of this tree are also grown in gardens. Northeastern USA south of the Great Lakes.

Crab apples are too hard and sour to eat raw, but are very good when preserved whole or pureed and eaten with a meat course. They can also be used to make excellent jelly or made into wine or cider.

The similar Prairie Crab Apple is common further west. Southern Crab Apple grows in the south east. Their fruits can be used in the same ways.

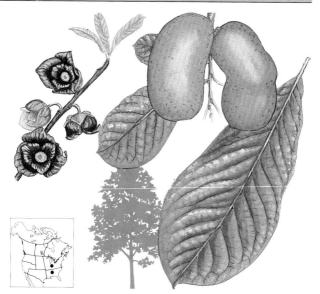

A small tree or shrub, up to 30ft tall, with gray-blotched brown, smooth bark and large deciduous leaves. Bell-shaped flowers have three small inner and three large outer, green or brown-purple, thick petals. Large fruits are cylindrical, slightly curved, green at first, turning brown when ripe.

Found in moist soils in bottomlands and river valleys, in mixed deciduous forests. Eastern USA except the far north and south, west into Kansas.

The banana-like fruits can be gathered before they are ripe and left to ripen in a cool place, or they can be picked when ripe. The flesh of the fruits is sweet and custard-like and can be eaten raw or cooked. To cook, remove seeds and skin, and use pulp in puddings or breads.

Pawpaw fruits may disagree with some people. Dwarf Pawpaw grows in southeastern USA. It also has edible fruits but only grows up to 4ft tall, and has smaller leaves and flowers.

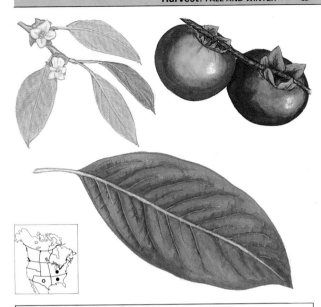

A tree with a dense rounded crown, up to 70ft tall, with shiny, dark green leaves and white, sweetly scented, bell-shaped flowers borne singly at the base of the leaves. Fruits are rounded, orange to purple-brown, soft and juicy when ripe, sour when unripe. Four woody sepals persist on the fruit.

Found in old fields, woodland margins, along roadsides and fence ways, in forest clearings and in bottomlands. Eastern USA, south from Connecticut and west to Missouri.

The fruits ripen in early fall but they are very sour until after the first frost. When ready to eat they are very soft and the skin is wrinkled. Eat fresh or use in fruit puddings, breads and pies. They can also be made into jam or frozen. The leaves can be steeped in boiling water to make tea.

Introduced persimmons are cultivated for their fruits. Texas Persimmon has edible black fruits that stain mouth and hands; it grows in southern Texas and Mexico.

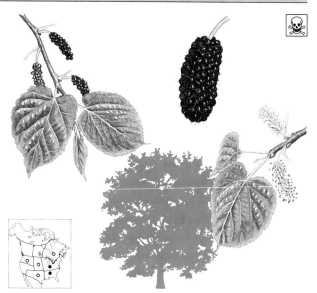

This 70ft tall tree has a rounded crown, dark red-brown bark and milky sap. Deciduous leaves are dull, dark green, heart-shaped or with two or three lobes. Male and female flowers grow in separate spikes on same tree. Fruits are cylindrical, dense clusters of tiny, sweet, juicy, red-purple berries.

Found in mixed deciduous woods in rich moist soil, in river valleys and on hillside slopes. Eastern USA except the far north. Also planted elsewhere for its fruit.

Pick ripe fruits in summer, eat raw with cream or use in pies, cakes, jams or jellies. They can be crushed to make a good drink when mixed with lemon juice and sugar. Pick young shoots in spring and boil for 20 minutes before eating as a green vegetable. Raw shoots and unripe fruit contain a hallucinogen.

White Mulberry trees are introduced and widespread; their sweet white fruits are best dried like raisins.

HACKBERRY

Harvest: FALL

A rounded tree, up to 90ft tall, with shiny green, long-pointed, toothed leaves. Its smooth bark has corky warts. Small green male and female flowers grow on long stalks from the leaf axils. Fruits are bright red, single-seeded berries, borne on long stalks in the leaf axils.

Found in river valleys and deciduous forests on upland slopes. Also planted as a street tree. Central USA from N. Dakota to Oklahoma and east to the coast. Absent from north and south.

The berries are dry and sweet and can either be eaten fresh or dried in the sun or in an oven for storage. Dried fruits can be used in baking. Fresh fruits can also be made into jam.

There are several other hackberries with edible berries. Netleaf Hackberry is found in similar habitats in the southwest and southern prairie states.

Seeds are produced by plants as a means of reproduction. They are rich in carbohydrates, oils & proteins, food stores for the seedlings which would develop, if the seeds were not eaten.

Nuts are a special form of seeds produced by some trees. In the first 8 pages of this section we have included representatives of all the major nut-producing trees in N. America. Nuts can be eaten raw, ground into meal or pressed to extract their oils. They may be salted or candied, used in pies & cakes, mixed with cereals or added to salads.

Many plants produce edible seeds. They may be eaten raw or roasted, ground into flour, added to cereals, used as a seasoning or in baking. Some are eaten as vegetables. Plants with edible seeds may be found on pages 108–112 of this section.

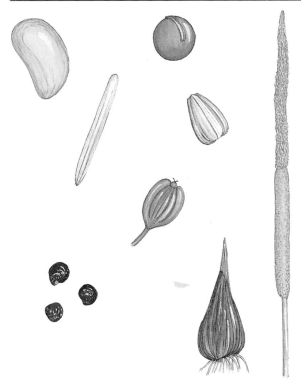

Plants in other sections of this book, which have edible seeds include:
Squaw-root (p. 17)
Groundnut (p. 28)
Peppergrass (p. 33)
Pickerelweed (p. 36)
Purslane (p. 38)
Pigweed (p. 44)
Lamb's Quarters (p. 45)
Wild Mustard (p. 51)
Cow Parsnip (p. 53)

Some plants are difficult to categorize, since so many parts are edible. Cat-tail is one such important multiple use plant. Others, like Sugar Maple which is used for its sap, or Wild Onion, which is used for its bulbs, do not fall clearly into any of the other sections of this book. Such plants have been included on pages 113–121.

A large tree, 60–80ft tall, with a narrow or spreading crown and thin, light gray bark. The deciduous, alternate leaves are leathery in texture, with toothed edges. Male and female flowers are tiny. Prickly round fruits split open in late summer to reveal two or three shiny brown triangular nuts.

Found in mixed deciduous woodland on rich moist soils, on lower mountain slopes and bottomlands. Eastern USA and southeastern Canada, west to the Great Lakes and Arkansas.

The nuts may be harvested as they fall from the trees after frost. Separate them from their prickly burrs and remove their shells, by heating them in an oven and rubbing them. They may be eaten raw, roasted, used in pies or ground into flour. Roasted nuts can be used as an excellent coffee substitute.

No similar edible species.

AMERICAN HAZELNUT

Harvest: SUMMER AND FALL

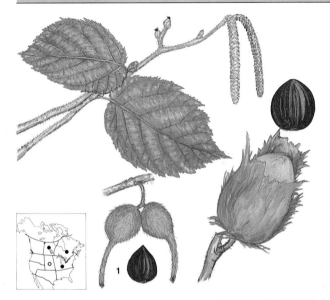

A large rounded shrub, up to 15ft tall, with hairy, glandular twigs and large deciduous leaves. The leaves have broad bases and pointed tips and sharp double teeth. Male catkins appear in early spring. Tiny female flowers are followed by hard-shelled nuts, partly cupped in two ragged leaf-like bracts.

Found in woods and thickets in northeastern USA, west to N. Dakota and across the border into southern Canada.

Hazelnuts can be gathered in late summer and fall. They must be removed from their shells and can then be eaten raw or used in nut recipes. They can be ground or roasted.

Beaked Hazelnut (1) has thin-shelled nuts enclosed in two bristly, beaklike, leafy bracts. It grows in the northern USA, from coast to coast, in woods on hills and slopes.

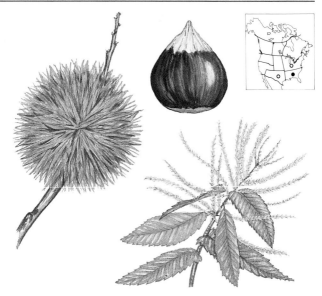

A small tree or large rounded shrub, up to 25ft tall. It has alternately arranged, 6in long, toothed leaves, green above, white-hairy beneath. Flowers grow in spikes, a few female flowers at the base, male flowers along the rest of the spike. Spiny burr-like fruits contain a single shiny dark brown nut.

Found in dry soils, in mixed oak and hickory woods, along mountain slopes and along the coast. Eastern USA, from eastern Texas north and east to Maryland.

Gather the nuts as they fall in late summer and fall and remove the spiny burrs. To remove shells, boil them until the shell can be removed. Nuts can be roasted, then eaten whole or ground to make coffee. They can be used in any chestnut recipe, in pies, stuffings, soups, as a vegetable or candied.

American Chestnuts are larger and sweeter but trees rarely produce fruits, since most are reduced to sprout-producing stumps by chestnut blight.

BLACK WALNUT

Harvest: FALL

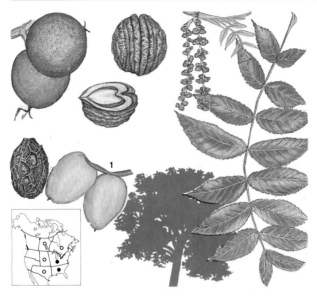

A large tree, up to 90ft tall, with an open crown and thick, furrowed, dark brown bark. It has large, deciduous, compound leaves with 15–23 saw-toothed leaflets. Greenish male catkins and small female flowers appear in spring. Fruits have thick green or brown husks covering hard-shelled nuts.

Found scattered in mixed forests, in moist bottomlands and floodplains, along streams, especially in well-drained soils. Eastern USA, except in north and south, west to Kansas.

Gather nuts early in fall, before they are eaten by squirrels. Remove husks by scrubbing, then break shells to obtain nuts. These may be eaten raw or pickled. Oil is produced by boiling crushed nuts. Nuts may also be ground for nut butter or used in any other walnut recipe.

Butternut is a related tree with egg-shaped fruits (**1**). These can be used in the same way, as can the nuts of the Californian Walnut. **Pecans** and some **Hickory** nuts are also edible.

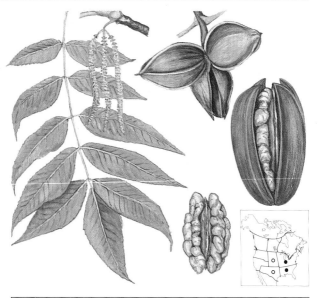

A large domed tree, up to 100ft tall, with furrowed red-brown bark. Deciduous, compound leaves have 9–17 toothed leaflets. Male catkins and small female flowers appear with the leaves. Fruits grow in clusters of 3–6; each has a dark brown husk which splits into four sections to reveal a thin-shelled nut.

Found in bottomlands and floodplains, in moist soils in southeastern and central eastern USA. Also extensively planted elsewhere for its nuts and its wood.

Gather nuts as leaves begin to fall. Pecan pie is a favorite use for these nuts but they can also be eaten raw or used in any recipe calling for walnuts. They can be made into candies, made into nut butter or boiled for their oil. Sap can be extracted from the tree in spring and used like maple sap.

The nuts from **Shagbark Hickory**, Shellbark Hickory, **Butternut** and **Walnut** can be used in the same ways. Some hickories have bitter nuts.

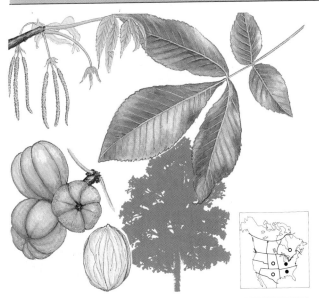

A large tree, up to 100ft tall, with gray, shaggy bark. The deciduous leaves have five finely-toothed hairy leaflets. Male catkins and tiny female flowers appear before leaves. Fruits have thick four-lobed husks, becoming dark brown and splitting into four sections to reveal light brown, thin-shelled nuts.

Found in mixed deciduous forests, in moist soils of upland slopes and valleys in much of eastern USA, west into Kansas, but absent from north and south. Also cultivated for its nuts.

Gather the nuts when they fall from the tree and remove husks and shells. Nuts can be eaten raw, candied or used in hickory pie. They can also be boiled for oil, when the nutmeats rise to the top — this is also a good way to separate nuts from shells. Sap can be used like maple sap.

Other hickories with sweet edible nuts are the **Pecan**, Mockernut and Shellbark Hickories; some hickories have bitter nuts. **Walnuts** and **Butternuts** can be used in the same ways.

WHITE OAK
Harvest: FALL

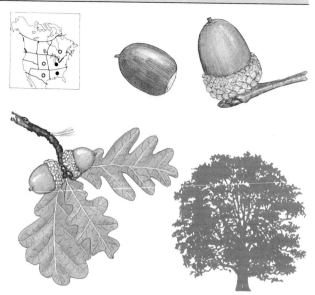

A large tree, up to 100ft tall, with widespread branches and light gray, fissured bark. The alternate, deciduous leaves are lobed but have no bristly tips on lobes. Light brown acorns grow on current year's twigs in a bowl-shaped cup enclosing a quarter of the acorn. Inside of acorn shell is not hairy.

Found in mixed and pure oak woods, often in moist soils, both in lowlands and on mountain slopes. Eastern USA, except far north and parts of south.

The white oak group of oaks has sweet acorns. Gather them as they fall from the trees. Store nuts in their shells. Before using remove shells, then grind coarsely and use like chopped nuts or grind finely for meal. Meal is excellent for muffins and pancakes. Roasted ground nuts make a good coffee substitute.

Many other oaks belong to this group including the Swamp Chestnut Oak, found in the east in moist soils and along streams; and the Gambel Oak of the Rocky Mountains.

NORTHERN RED OAK

Harvest: FALL

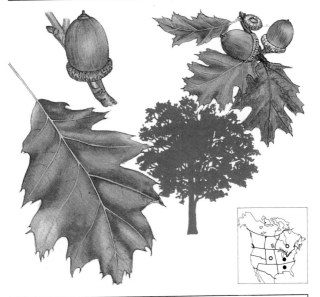

A large tree, up to 90ft tall, with spreading branches and rough, ridged, dark gray bark. Leaves are up to 9in long, lobed with bristly teeth tipping the lobes. Acorns grow on previous year's twigs in a saucer-shaped cup enclosing a quarter of the acorn. Inside of acorn shell is hairy.

Found on the lower and middle slopes and in the valleys of mountains on all kinds of soils, often forming pure stands. Eastern USA except the far south, and into eastern Canada.

The red oak group of oaks has bitter acorns. After gathering, they must be shelled and then soaked in repeated changes of boiling water until all the tannins are removed, i.e. until the water does not turn brown anymore. Then they can be used like white oak acorns.

Many other oaks belong to this group including the Black Oak, found in dry upland areas in the east, and the Tanoak of the mountains of California.

107

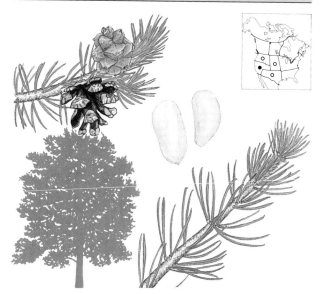

A small bushy pine tree, up to 30ft tall, with short, curving, light green needles growing in pairs. Cones are egg-shaped, yellow-brown and sticky; they open to release the large, wingless seeds which are sweet and oily and yellow-brown in color with red markings.

Found on the lower mountain slopes and foothills, in dry rocky places and canyons, in the Rocky Mountains of southwestern USA.

Gather cones just before they open in fall and dry so the scales will separate and release seeds. Or roast for 30 minutes — this improves the flavor of the seeds. Seeds may be eaten fresh or stored after roasting. They may also be ground into meal and mixed with flour for use in bread etc.

Several other western pines have edible seeds, including the Singleleaf Pinyon, Digger and Sugar Pines. Their cones may be difficult to obtain from the taller trees.

SUNFLOWER

Harvest: SUMMER AND FALL

Wild native plants are rough, branched annuals, up to 10ft tall, with large, rather pointed heart-shaped leaves, borne alternately. They have many flower heads, each about an inch across, with yellow ray florets and a reddish central disk. Flat seed-heads contain dry fruits, each with one seed.

Found on roadsides and in grasslands, especially on the prairies, but also throughout the USA and southern Canada.

Harvest the seed-heads in late summer and fall and hang them to dry in a warm dry place. The seeds need to be removed from their shells and can be eaten raw. They can be crushed and boiled for sunflower oil — skim the oil from the top. They can be ground, made into nut butter or added to flour.

There are many other species of sunflowers in North America. They all have edible seeds. **Jerusalem Artichoke** is a related plant with edible tubers.

WILD RICE
Harvest: SUMMER AND FALL

An annual grass, growing up to 10ft tall, with light green leaves. The flowers grow in large plumes with female flowers on erect terminal branches and male flowers on the spreading side branches; the flower stems are up to 2ft tall. The seeds are hard, brown and cylindrical and enclosed in papery husks.

An aquatic grass, found in marshes and along the margins of ponds, lakes, streams and rivers in eastern and northern USA and in the extreme southern areas of Canada.

Harvest the grains from a shallow boat, knocking the ripe grains into the boat, spread them to dry, then thresh and winnow to remove husks. Cook like cultivated brown rice or grind them into a flour and use in ground rice recipes.

Some grains may be replaced by the purple fruiting bodies of the fungus, Ergot, which is very poisonous. Do not eat affected grains.

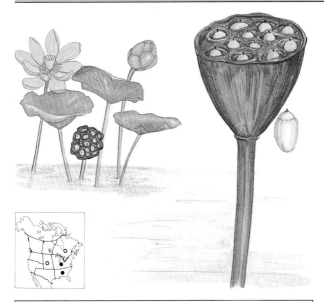

Perennial aquatic plant with swollen tuber-like roots embedded in the mud, and circular, bowl-shaped, blue-green leaves growing on long stalks above the water. The large, showy, pale yellow flowers are followed by fruits in receptacles like large showerheads. The fruits are hard and nut-like.

Found in quiet lakes, ponds and slow-moving rivers in both fresh and brackish waters, in eastern USA.

Ripe fruits can be cracked to extract seeds, and the seeds can be roasted and eaten like nuts or ground into flour. Fresh seeds can be boiled and eaten like chestnuts. Young shoots can be used like spinach. Harvesting the roots is difficult but they can be used like sweet potatoes.

Yellow Pond Lilies also have edible, potato-like tubers and edible seeds. They have shiny green, cleft leaves raised above the water surface, yellow flowers and urn-shaped fruits.

A low-growing perennial plant, with trailing stems up to 3ft long. The pinnate leaves have 6–10 leaflets and end in tendrils; there are two large triangular stipules at the base of each leaf. The usually purple, pea-like flowers grow in small sprays and are followed by pods of small peas.

Found on the beaches of the east coast south to New Jersey; the west coast south to Calif.; also along the shores of the Great Lakes and a few other lakes in northeastern USA.

Harvest the peas while they are still tender, small and bright green. Cook in boiling water for about 15 minutes, serve with butter. Like garden peas, these vegetables are high in protein and vitamins.

West coast Beach Peas have purple flowers with white wings and white keel. Avoid the peas of other wild pea species as they are poisonous.

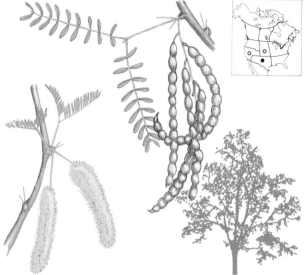

A thicket-forming tree, up to 25ft tall, with a pair of sharp thorns at the base of each leaf. The deciduous compound leaves are featherlike, with 14–18 bright green leaflets on two forks. Yellow flowers grow in narrow clusters and are followed by long narrow pods, constricted between the seeds.

Found in desert washes and valleys, in open range and grassland, in sandy ground, sandhills and deserts. Southwestern USA from Texas to California.

The mature pods contain a sweet, gelatinous pulp around the bean-like seeds. The pods can be eaten fresh or dried and ground to make meal. They can also be boiled to make a drink or fermented. The flowers are rich in nectar and can be sucked.

Screwbean Mesquite, from the same area, has spirally twisted pods; immature pods can be cooked as a vegetable or boiled down to make syrup.

PRICKLY PEAR OR INDIAN FIG

Harvest: SPRING TO FALL

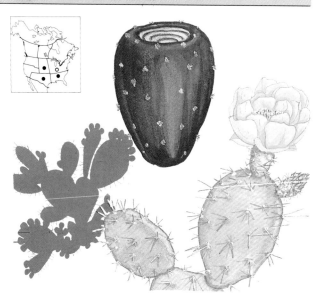

This plant forms clumps of flattened, jointed, sprawling stems, up to 3ft tall; the segments are nearly circular. Stems are studded with red-brown bumps of tiny barbed hairs. Flowers are yellow with red centers. The fleshy, barbed fruits are reddish-brown, with many circular, flattened seeds.

Found in dry soils, in dry, sandy grasslands, on sand dunes and amongst rocks. Minnesota south to Oklahoma and S. Dakota. Other edible prickly pears are found in the west.

Wear protective gloves to cut young segments. Flame segments to remove barbs, they can be roasted and peeled, or peeled, cut into strips and cooked like string beans. The pulp of the fruits can be eaten fresh — remove the seeds and beware barbs on your skin.

All flattened species of prickly pears can be eaten in the same way. The majority of prickly pears are found in the dry areas of the south and south west.

114

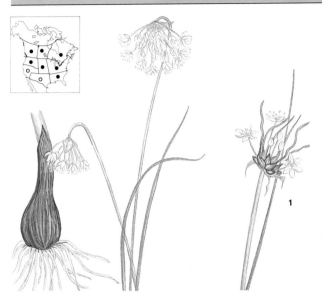

A bulbous plant with a reddish purple bulb, from which grows a clump of thin, flattened grass-like leaves, up to 2ft tall, and several flower stalks. The white or pink flowers are produced in terminal nodding clusters and are followed by more erect fruits. The whole plant smells of onions.

Found in open woodland, rocky slopes, prairies and dry meadows throughout southern Canada and the USA except Calif. There are also many other onion species found throughout the continent.

Use bulbs in spring and fall for pickles, for onion soup, in salads, or boil or cream them as a vegetable. Young tops can be cut before the flowers appear, to use in salads. **Wild Garlic (1)** can be used in the same ways, and the bulblets in the flower clusters make good pickles.

Wild Onion is the most widespread of the onion species, and one of the most palatable. There are many others which can be used in the same ways but some are very strongly flavored.

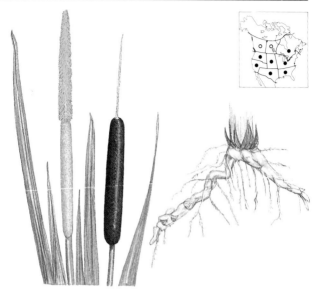

From creeping stems grow stands of 9ft tall, sword-like leaves; the leaves have sheathed bases. The flowers grow in dense cylindrical spikes on tall upright stems, yellow male flowers above and green female ones below. They are followed by cigar-shaped fruits which break up into soft downy seeds.

Found growing in dense stands in the shallow water margins of lakes and ponds and in marshes; they also grow in ditches and beside slow-moving rivers. Throughout the USA and Canada.

Spring buds on underground stems and young shoots can be eaten raw or cooked like asparagus. Cores of the young leaves can be cooked in the same way. Cook female flowers like corn on the cob and use ripe pollen as a flour substitute. Starchy cores of underground stems in winter can also be ground into flour.

Narrow-leaved Cat-tail can be used in the same ways. The stems and leaves of Wild Irises are poisonous — they can be recognized by their showy flowers and capsule-like fruits.

Harvest: ALL YEAR

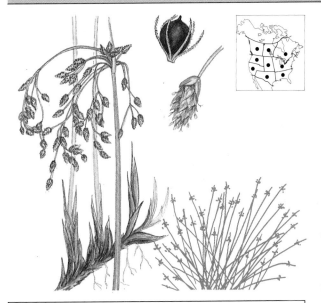

A perennial plant that forms scaly reddish underground stems, from which grow many soft green stems, up to 10ft tall. It has no leaves. The bristly, brown flowers are borne on several branched flower stalks forming a dense cluster near the tip of each stem. The fruits are hard and flattened.

Found on the margins of lakes, ponds, rivers and streams, and in marshes throughout the USA and Canada, except the far north.

Young shoots can be eaten raw in salads, boiled or roasted. Use the cores of the young leaves in the same way. Young sections of underground stems can be roasted and eaten like potatoes. Flour can be made by pounding the older roots or by boiling them into a gruel. Use pollen as a flour supplement.

There are several other common widespread bulrushes which can be used in the same ways.

SPICEBUSH
Harvest: ALL YEAR

A tall shrub, up to 15ft high, with many smooth, more or less upright branches, simple deciduous, bright green leaves and a spicy scent. Dense clusters of small yellow flowers appear in spring before the leaves and are followed by clusters of oval, spicy berries, green at first, later turning bright red.

Found in damp woods and along streams in eastern USA and into eastern Canada.

Gather the young leaves in spring, fresh twigs and bark during the rest of the year, and use them to make tea. Steep the fresh leaves or twigs in boiling water and add milk and sugar to taste. The berries can be dried in an oven and ground as a substitute for allspice.

There are no similar edible species. The roots of the related **Sassafras** can be used to make tea.

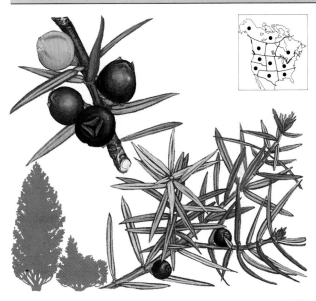

Evergreen conifers, usually large spreading shrubs or small upright trees. Their branches have thin bark which often shreds in longitudinal strips. They have two kinds of leaves; young needle-like ones, arranged in threes and mature scale-like ones. The fruits are small fleshy, berry-like cones.

There are over a dozen species of junipers in N. America, more species occurring in the west than the east. They are most likely to be found in dry rocky habitats.

Only a few junipers have edible fruits. The ripe berries may be gathered from late summer to winter. Even those considered edible are high in resins and, although sweet, are not very good raw. When ground, they form an excellent seasoning for roast meats or may be used as a coffee substitute.

Common Juniper (illustrated) grows throughout the continent; it varies from a narrow upright shrub to a ground-hugging form. The Rocky Mountain Juniper has edible blue berries.

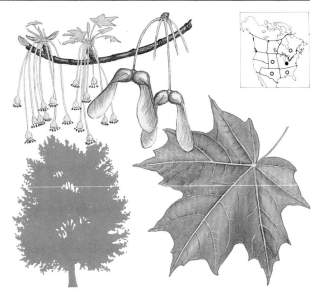

A large domed tree, up to 100ft tall, with rough gray bark. It has thin, palmate leaves, the lobes long-pointed and toothed. Leaves turn yellow, red and orange in fall. Drooping clusters of yellow-green flowers appear with the leaves. Propeller-like fruits are pale green to brown, with slightly spreading wings.

Found in deciduous upland forests and on lower mountain slopes, often in pure stands. Northeastern USA and into southern Canada, west to Minnesota and south to Tennessee.

Collect sap when days are warm and nights still freezing. Boil sap outdoors, in a wide open pan to make maple syrup. Several gallons and accurate temperature measurements are needed to make one pint of syrup. Continue boiling to make maple sugar. Unripe seeds may be shelled, boiled and roasted in summer.

The sap of all native maples may be used in the same way but all the others have a low sugar content in their sap.

S

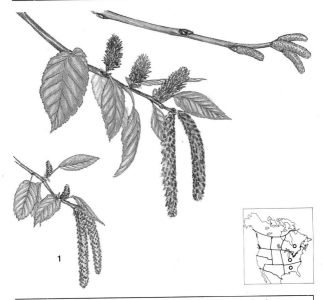

1

A rounded tree, 70–80ft tall, with peeling red-brown bark, turning gray or yellow-brown. Leaves are simple and edged with sharp double teeth. Winter twigs bear alternate, pointed, long, brown, somewhat sticky buds with terminal clusters of new male catkins. Broken twigs smell slightly of wintergreen.

Found in rich, damp woods and lower slopes of hills, usually below 1000ft; sometimes in marshes. Northeastern USA and eastern Canada.

The copious sap can be harvested in the spring, in the same way as maple sap, and made into syrup, although its sugar content is lower. The inner bark can be ground into flour in spring. The twigs and leaves can be steeped in water to make tea at any time. Sweet Birch twigs and leaves make better tea.

Sweet or **Black Birch** (**1**), from the moist cool forests of northeastern USA, has smooth, red or almost black bark and its twigs smell of wintergreen. It can be used in the same way.

Index and check-list

All species in Roman type are illustrated.
Keep a record of your sightings by checking the boxes.